Java Unit Testing with JUnit 5

Test Driven Development
with JUnit 5

Shekhar Gulati
Rahul Sharma

Apress®

Java Unit Testing with JUnit 5

Shekhar Gulati
Gurgaon, Haryana, India

Rahul Sharma
Delhi, Delhi, India

ISBN-13 (pbk): 978-1-4842-3014-5
https://doi.org/10.1007/978-1-4842-3015-2

ISBN-13 (electronic): 978-1-4842-3015-2

Library of Congress Control Number: 2017959333

Cover image designed by Freepik

Managing Director: Welmoed Spahr
Editorial Director: Todd Green
Acquisitions Editor: Nikhil Karkal
Development Editor: James Markham and Priyanka Mehta
Technical Reviewer: Ashwani Kumar
Coordinating Editor: Prachi Mehta
Copy Editor: Lori Jacobs
Compositor: SPi Global
Indexer: SPi Global
Artist: SPi Global

Distributed to the book trade worldwide by Springer Science+Business Media New York, 233 Spring Street, 6th Floor, New York, NY 10013. Phone 1-800-SPRINGER, fax (201) 348-4505, e-mail orders-ny@springer-sbm.com, or visit www.springeronline.com. Apress Media, LLC is a California LLC and the sole member (owner) is Springer Science + Business Media Finance Inc (SSBM Finance Inc). SSBM Finance Inc is a **Delaware** corporation.

For information on translations, please e-mail rights@apress.com, or visit http://www.apress.com/rights-permissions.

Apress titles may be purchased in bulk for academic, corporate, or promotional use. eBook versions and licenses are also available for most titles. For more information, reference our Print and eBook Bulk Sales web page at http://www.apress.com/bulk-sales.

Any source code or other supplementary material referenced by the author in this book is available to readers on GitHub via the book's product page, located at www.apress.com/978-1-4842-3014-5. For more detailed information, please visit http://www.apress.com/source-code.

Printed on acid-free paper

Contents at a Glance

Contents

About the Authors

Shekhar Gulati is Chief Technology Evangelist at Xebia. For the last couple of years, he has worked on building a deployment automation tool. Before that, he worked as a technology evangelist for Red Hat, speaking and writing about the cloud computing ecosystem. He has authored two popular writing series: https://github.com/shekhargulati/52-technologies-in-2016 and https://shekhargulati.com/30-technologies-in-30-days/.

Rahul Sharma is a seasoned Java developer, author, and presenter. He has 12+ years of experience in building and designing applications on the Java/J2EE platforms. In his career, he has worked with companies of various sizes, from enterprises to startups. He is a practitioner of Agile and XP and clearly understands the process of software craftmanship. He is also an open source enthusiast and has contributed to a variety of open source projects such as Apache Crunch, Apache Provisionr, and Apache HDT. He is currently working as Development Manager with the Royal Bank of Scotland.

About the Technical Reviewer

Ashwani Kumar holds a B-tech degree from NIT Allahabad in Information Technology and has a total of nine plus years of experience.

He is a software developer with extensive experience in developing highly scalable back-end systems on the cloud. Ashwani has developed applications in wide range of languages including Java, C#, JavaScript, and Python. He is also a self-taught Android developer who loves to share his learnings via his blog (`http://blog.ashwanik.in`). In his free time, he also tries his hand at machine learning and artificial intelligence.

CHAPTER 1

■ ■ ■

Building Software the Correct Way

Programmers learn very quickly that writing software is hard and error prone. Time and again software projects fail because teams are unable to cope with software complexity. As a result, the project fails to meet the deadline, costs much more than expected, and doesn't deliver the intended business value.

If we look back, software programming as a profession is only a few decades old. In its short lifespan, we have seen multiple software development processes and discovered a few best practices. We have learned that like any other evolutionary process, software also evolves over time. Thus, we should adapt to change rather than stick to a strict plan. We have also discovered that development is a collaborative process—many individuals work on different parts of the software to build something that meets customer needs. Different individuals perform different roles iteratively to determine a product's future. Many organizations are embracing the Agile software development process to help them cope with the ever-changing business requirements. As they say, *the only constant is change*.

Test-driven development (TDD) is one of the practices of Agile software development that a lot of developers use in some shape or form. The premise of TDD is that you write a failing test case before you write the production code itself. TDD, if done correctly, can help you write software that meets customer expectations, has a simple design, and has fewer defects.

In this chapter, we will help you understand why, as a professional programmer, you should learn and follow TDD practices. You will learn how to set up a Gradle-based Java 8 JUnit 5 project. We will provide a short primer of new features in Java 8 so that you feel at home in case you have not worked with Java 8 before. We will end the chapter by writing a simple example following TDD practice. This chapter will prepare you for future chapters in which we will use TDD to build a fully working application and demonstrate advance features of JUnit 5.

© Shekhar Gulati, Rahul Sharma 2017
S. Gulati, R. Sharma, *Java Unit Testing with JUnit 5*,
https://doi.org/10.1007/978-1-4842-3015-2_1

Test-Driven Development

Do you remember the last time you wanted to make a change to fix a critical defect that a customer discovered? Were you certain that your fix would not introduce a regression error? Also, think about the last time you wanted to refactor your code but you feared that your change might break something else? This happens a lot in software development–the fear of breaking software. Even the best programmers make mistakes and introduce defects.

Software projects involve a lot of uncertainties. We work with new technologies, ever-changing requirements, people movement, or a combination of these. To overcome the fear and manage these uncertainties, we need a software development practice that can help us produce working software. It must keep things simple and provide us quick feedback in case things go wrong.

Test-driven development, rediscovered by Kent Beck in 2003, is a development practice that increases developer confidence by advocating tests for all software requirements. It makes us work in short (a few minutes) incremental development cycles, thus providing quick feedback on our progress. TDD forces us to write a failing test before writing the production code. The complete process looks as follows:

1. Add a test for the new functionality or behavior.

2. See it fail.

3. Write enough code to make the test pass.

4. Make sure all the previous tests pass as well.

5. Refactor the code.

6. Repeat until done.

The key part here is writing a failing test first. The test specifies our understanding of the system. We are writing what we expect the system will do when some action is performed. This helps us to clearly understand the system.

This book will focus on the test-first approach of TDD. There are many programmers who write test last. We think the test-last approach does not help you achieve the full benefit of TDD. TDD is sometimes called test-driven design (i.e., tests should help you to design the system). The design part of TDD is more important than the testing part. When we do test last, we don't reap the design benefit from the practice.

In software development, quick feedback is the key to software productivity. TDD gives us quick feedback that we are moving in the right direction. In a way, it keeps our mind focused and positive. We believe in our code as it is meeting end user expectations written in tests.

TDD helps us achieve two important goals:

- Detect regression errors.

- Keep system design simple.

Let's discuss each of these aspects in detail.

Detect Regression Errors

The most obvious reason to follow TDD is to detect regression errors in an automated manner. Teams that follow TDD have the freedom to change and add new features without worrying about introducing regressions. If all the previous test cases ran fine, then we can be sure that we have not introduced any regression error. Also, as we keep adding tests for the new behavior the safety net keeps growing. These test cases pay off each time someone makes a change. The sooner we detect a bug in the code, the faster and cheaper it is to fix. This is validated by the data shared by Google which you can see in Table 1-1.

Table 1-1. Cost to Fix Bugs

Software Testing Phase Where Bug Found	Estimate Cost per Bug
System Test	$5,000
Integration Test	$500
Full Build	$50
Unit Test/Test-Driven Development	$5

Some people may not see value in writing tests. They prefer to test the code manually or to use log statements to debug code when things go wrong. The act of testing manually is cumbersome and time-consuming. Besides this, it is difficult to manually cover all the corner cases of any nontrivial software. Humans are usually good at checking the happy paths (i.e., scenarios which always work). So, there is a great possibility that manual testing will miss some corner cases.

If the system is written following TDD, then any time you discover a bug, the team will add an additional test case that reproduces the error. Now, you will be able to make changes to the production code to pass the failing test case. This will ensure that the corner case is handled. Also, as this corner case is now part of the automated test suite you can be rest assured that you will not miss it again.

Keep System Design Simple

Automated tests written by programmers have traditionally been considered a quality assurance effort. They are targeted at verifying the correctness of an implementation at the time of writing and verifying its correctness in the future as the code evolves. Testing is only one-half of the story. We will demonstrate, throughout this book, that TDD is essentially a design tool and testing is just a side effect.

One of the ways people look at software development is by breaking it into different phases. The two most common phases are

- Design

- Coding

Often, one team designs the system and another team implements it. When people try to implement a design created by others, it often does not work. Programmers face many challenges when they start implementing the proposed design.

TDD breaks the myth of seperate design and coding phase by promoting the idea that code is design. We don't need a big upfront design that always falls short when we implement stuff. We need a just-in-time design that will evolve as the system is built.

When we start writing tests, we start to design the code with a caller in the mind. Tests become client of the code. Tests help us write just enough code to meet the required behavior. Once we have a passing test, we mercilessly refactor the code. TDD is often looked as a continuous cycle of RED -> GREEN -> REFACTOR. It is the refactoring stage where design emerges. Refactoring is defined as improving the design of existing code without changing its external behavior. Tests help us gain confidence that our code works as expected. Now, we can safely refactor the code. In case, we make a breaking change during the refactoring, the test case will fail. Hence, saving us from introducing an unintended side effect while refactoring.

The refactoring phase of TDD is the most critical phase. While refactoring, think about Boy Scout Code of Conduct:

Always leave the campground cleaner than you found it.

Refactoring does not mean you have to make your code perfect. Try to make the code little better than when you first checked it out. You can improve the name of a variable, method, or class. You can break a big function into smaller functions or extract out a concern to a different class. The goal is to make the current version better than the previous version. If we follow this practice each day we will move toward simpler readable code base.

TDD as a design tool requires a change in mind-set. It will not happen in a day. It takes constant practice to master and reap the benefits.

TDD forces us to write loosely coupled classes so that we can easily test them in isolation. We are forced to make dependencies explicit to test the specific code in isolation. We write small cohesive modules that do one thing so that we can test specific behaviors. The modules can be extended in the future to meet changing requirements. These are all good design practices enforced by TDD. This all makes reading and understanding code much easier. Various studies tell us that programmers spend more time reading and understanding code than writing it. In 2007, Microsoft conducted a survey where 95% of respondents agreed that understanding existing code is a significant part of their job.

Levels of Testing

As you start practicing TDD, you will write different levels of tests. Your application should be composed of tests in each of the following levels. Each of these levels focuses on a different aspect of code and provides different feedback. Let's look at them one by one.

- Unit testing: Here you test individual software components to verify if the individual unit does the right thing in isolation.

- Integration testing: Here you test multiple units together to verify if they work correctly as a unit.

- Acceptance testing: Here you test the full system to verify if it works as per user expectations. It is often referred to as functional testing.

Figure 1-1 depicts a test pyramid. The point Figure 1-1 conveys is that you should have many more unit tests than functional or integration tests. This book will mainly focus on unit testing, but you should spend time learning about the other two types of tests as well.

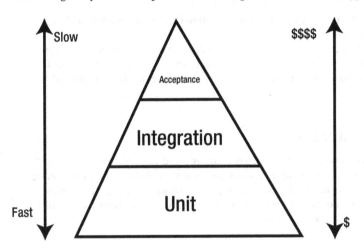

Figure 1-1. *Test pyramid*

The unit testing concept dates back to 1976 when David J. Panzal presented *Test Procedures: A New Approach to Software Verification* at the second international conference on software engineering. The paper describes *test procedure* as a way to invoke a *test case* on a *target module* to generate a report indicating whether the "test case" has failed. These *test procedures* are part of product deliverables and can be used as initial product validation and subsequent regression testing. These procedures were written for FORTRAN in a language called Test Procedure language (TPL)

Benefits of Unit Testing

As discussed previously, unit testing is no longer a post-development exercise. It is as equally important as writing production code and must be done up front. It enhances team productivity by providing solid foundations. Let's look at the benefits unit testing offers in detail.

Determines Specifications

Before we start the journey of coding a component we must try to determine what the component must do? Try to build a test case of the possible inputs and the possible outputs. The act of building test cases at the start helps to clarify the expected behavior of the component.

If we are unable to come up with a test, it means that the specifications are not explicit enough and require more thinking.

Provides Early Error Detection

Unit tests are proof of working code. They are executed in every build and can detect failures at the first instance.

Unit tests can detect not only coding bugs but flaws in product specifications as well. A unit test demonstrates progress; thus, as soon as a component is complete, it can be demo-ed to the stakeholders to find gaps, if any. The sooner a bug is uncovered, the cheaper it is to fix.

Supports Maintenance

Product specifications evolve over time. These changes lead to development cycles. In each of these cycles, the team has to understand how the existing code works before team members can make any changes. Unit tests help in understanding the intended behavior without being bogged down by the actual code. A well-written unit test suite serves as a productivity boost for the team.

Improves Design

Unit tests are the first client of the code being tested. They uncover various issues that a client can face while interfacing with the code being tested. Unit tests make us think in terms of the expected input and the expected output. For internal components (service, utilities, etc.), this can help in classifying responsibility boundaries. It helps in improving product specifications by exposing gaps in the interface design.

Product Documentation

Unit tests describe how a piece of code works—that is, the expected output for a given input. They always describe the latest state of a specification, as they are kept in sync with the code changes.

Characteristics of Good Unit Tests

Tests should be written with the same focus and clarity as the production code. We must refactor test cases so that they are kept lean and correct. Tests will only reap benefits if people can understand and rely on them.

When following TDD, high-quality tests are the key to success. It's one thing merely to have tests, and another thing to have high-quality tests. The tests need to have several characteristics so that they remain useful throughout their life. They should be

- **Readable**: One of the goals of a test is to educate its reader about what the unit being tested will do. If the tests are not readable then the reader will not be able to understand when the tests will fail. A good unit test case has a meaningful name so that the reader understands the behavior of unit being tested without looking at implementation details.

- **Fast**: Tests should run in few seconds so that they provide quick feedback. If tests take more time, the programmer will look for ways to skip the tests. Unit tests must mock external dependencies so that the tests run fast and independent of external services. Mocking allows testing of a unit of code by simulating behaviour of its dependencies in a controlled manner.

- **Independent and Isolated**: Good unit tests are independent of execution order. They don't rely on other unit tests for them to work correctly. They should run independently in their own isolated environment.

- **Correct**: A good unit test does what it says. A test case should correspond to a single case (i.e., behavior). Often tests don't do what their name suggests. This is very risky, as in that case you can't trust your tests.

- **Environment agnostic**: A litmus test for any software project is the following: "Can you check out the code on a clean developer machine and run the full build including tests without any problem." Most of the time, we find that unit tests fail because they depend on some external factor. The external factor could be a file at a particular location, an environment variable, or something else. This leads to brittle tests. A good unit test does not depend on the environment.

- **Repeatable**: A good unit test produces the same result each time you run it. Test execution should be automated using the build tool. They should be part of the automated build process so that they run each time you execute build. When tests start failing randomly, programmers start ignoring them. These random test failures are difficult to reproduce and normally happen on external systems like continuous integration servers. Team should ensure that failing tests are fixed as soon as they are discovered.

JUnit Introduction

JUnit, developed by Kent Beck and Erich Gamma, is one of the most popular unit-testing frameworks for Java developers. It was originally based on SUnit, a unit-testing framework written in Smalltalk (developed by Kent Beck). The first version of JUnit was released in 1997. It has since become the de facto standard, adopted in many different languages and by many tools. **Martin Fowler** highlights the importance of JUnit framework in his quote:

> *Never in the field of software development have so many owed so much to so few lines of code.*

Prior to the introduction of JUnit, testing discipline was dominated by *capture and replay* testing tools. These tools were black-box testing tools, which used to capture the state of the system with a given input and then try to replay it. The tests written in such a framework involved an enormous amount of effort. These tools were not designed to unit test a component as they tested the application using its graphical user interface (GUI).

JUnit rejected the idea of GUI-based tests. It instead provided a lightweight framework, which enabled test creation by writing code in Java. This allowed developers to build test suites for every piece of their code. Due to its benefits, JUnit was integrated with all kinds of build tools and integrated development environments (IDEs).

The JUnit team has been adept at utilizing the new Java language features. Post the release of Java 5, which enabled the use of annotations, generics, and so on, JUnit 4.0 was released with features like @Test, and @Setup. **Kent Beck** said the following about JUnit 4:

> *The theme of JUnit 4 is to encourage more developers to write more tests by further simplifying JUnit.*

JUnit 4.0 simplified unit testing by getting away from naming conventions and introducing several other features like timeouts and test exceptions. JUnit 4.0 was released a decade ago, sometime in February 2006. Throughout the next ten years, we have seen multiple minor releases of JUnit, with the latest being JUnit 4.12, which was released in December 2014. Before we learn more about JUnit 5, let's understand why we need a new version of JUnit framework.

Why We Need a New Version of JUnit?

As developer testing gained momentum and maturity over the last few years, developers began to expect more from their unit-testing framework. Following are the reasons a new version was required:

- **Features**: Developers want their testing framework to support integration testing, better assertions, and many other features so that they don't have to rely on other libraries.

- **Modularity**: Earlier versions of JUnit lack modularity. Everything is packaged as one single jar. There is a single JUnit project, which contains all JUnit code base. It achieves modularity by using different subpackages. This means everyone is dependent on JUnit jar—build tools, IDE, your JUnit tests, extensions, and so on, all using the same code. Test discovery and test execution are one example of concern regarding tight coupling.

- **Extensibility**: JUnit 4 provided extensibility using two mechanisms:

  - Runner API (application programming interface)

  - Rule API

  They both had their strengths and limitations. To write a custom test runner, you have to implement the complete test life cycle, which includes test instantiation, test execution, setup and teardown, and so on. The biggest drawback of Runner API is that you can't combine multiple runners together.

  Rule API introduced in JUnit 4.7 is much simpler to work with but is limited in what it can do. One limitation of Rule API was that there couldn't be a single rule for both method-level and class-level callbacks. This left a lot from JUnit in terms of extensibility.

- **Java 8**: Java 8 introduces a lot of new features like lambdas. You can use Java 8 with previous versions of JUnit, but JUnit itself can be improved a lot by supporting these features.

JUnit 5

To overcome the limitations mentioned previously, JUnit Lambda project was initiated. JUnit Lambda was the code name for JUnit 5. JUnit 5 is a complete rewrite of JUnit in Java 8. You need Java 8 to use JUnit 5. It is redesigned from the ground up, overcoming the mistakes and limitations of previous JUnit versions. This does not mean that tests written in JUnit 3 and JUnit 4 will not work with JUnit 5. JUnit team has made sure that JUnit 5 is backward compatible, so you can run your old JUnit tests with it as well. JUnit 5 supports JUnit 3.8 and above versions.

JUnit 5 is composed of three subprojects. Each of these subprojects has multiple modules, which we will look at later.

- **JUnit Platform**: This provides a foundation for launching JVM (Java Virtual Machine) testing frameworks. This includes a TestEngine API that can be used to develop a testing framework for JUnit Platform to run. It also provides a ConsoleLauncher that build tools like Gradle and Maven can use.

- **JUnit Jupiter**: This provides the new programming model for writing tests. Also, the new extension mechanism is part of this subproject. It implements the TestEngine API defined by JUnit Platform so that JUnit 5 tests can be run.

- **JUnit Vintage**: This provides a TestEngine implementation for running JUnit 3 and JUnit 4 tests.

JUnit 5 architecture looks as shown in Figure 1-2. JUnit 5 replaced the concept of runners with the engine. So, in the middle, there is an engine API that is implemented for both JUnit 4 and JUnit 5 API. This allows you to run tests written using different versions of JUnit. Tools like Gradle, IntelliJ, or Eclipse use the launcher API. Your tests will depend on the JUnit 5 API keeping you away from JUnit internals.

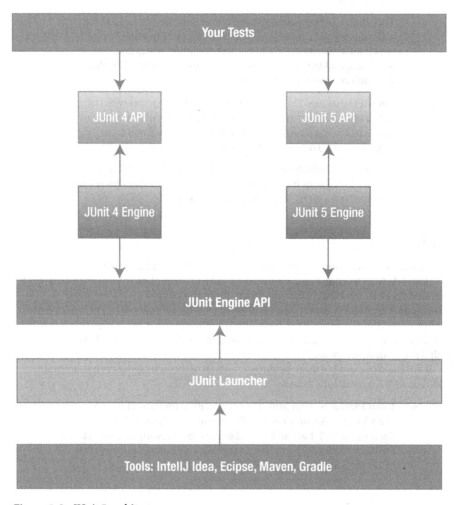

Figure 1-2. *JUnit 5 architecture*

The main modules in JUnit 5 are

- **junit-jupiter-api**: This module defines the API that you need to write your tests.

- **junit-platform-launcher**: This module defines the launcher API that external tool use. Launchers can be used to discover, filter, and execute tests.

- **junit-platform-engine**: This provides the API that you can use to write your own TestEngine. TestEngine is responsible for the discovery and execution of tests.

- **junit-jupiter-engine**: It is the implementation of junit-platform-engine API for JUnit 5.

- **junit-vintage-engine**: It is the implementation of junit-platform-engine API for JUnit 3 and JUnit 4.

- **junit-platform-commons**: It contains all the utilities which are used across different modules.

- **junit-platform-console**: This provides an implementation of a launcher called ConsoleLauncher. ConsoleLauncher is a stand-alone application used to launch JUnit platform from the console.

- **junit-platform-gradle-plugin**: This is a Gradle plug-in that can be used to run JUnit 5 tests.

- **junit-platform-surefire-provider**: This module provides Maven integration for JUnit 5.

JUnit team is also trying to build a strong foundation for testing tool providers and build tools/IDEs. In this version, they have launched an Open Test Alliance (https://github.com/ota4j-team/opentest4j), which is aimed at defining standards for test execution on JVM.

Java 8 Primer

Java 8 is not a new topic anymore. There have been many good books published on it. Still, many Java developers are unaware of the power of Java 8. Throughout this book, we will be using Java 8, so we will provide a short primer of important Java 8 features in this section.

Java 8 is the biggest release of Java to date. It comes packed with many features like lambdas, stream API, optional, new date-time API, default and static methods in interfaces, and many others. In this section, we will look at the three most important features of Java 8–lambdas, stream API, and optional—which will change the way we work with Java.

Lambdas

The most important feature introduced in Java 8 is lambda expressions. Lambda expressions allow you to pass behavior as data. In earlier versions of Java, we used anonymous inner classes for passing behavior. Let's look at a simple example of lambda expression–sort function in Java's Collections class. The sort function takes List and Comparator and sorts based on the provided Comparator.

```
List<String> books = Arrays.asList("Effective Java", "Clean Code", "Refactoring");
Collections.sort(books, (b1, b2) -> b1.length() - b2.length()));
```

The code snippet sorts book titles according to their length. The output of the program will be [Refactoring, Clean Code, Effective Java].

The expression `(b1, b2) -> b1.length() - b2.length()` shown in the code snippet is a lambda expression of type `Comparator<String>`.

- The `(b1, b2)` are parameters of the compare method of `Comparator`.

- `b1.length() - b2.length()` is the function body that compares the length of two book titles.

- `->` is the lambda operator that separates parameters from the body of the lambda.

Streams API

Streams provide a higher-level abstraction to express computations in Java collections in a declarative manner. It is similar to how you use SQL to declaratively query data in a database. Declarative means developers write what they want to do rather than specifying all the instructions on how the data should be queried. Streams only provide read-only operations. They never change the underlying collection.

Following is an example code snippet that does collection processing in Java 7:

```
public class ExampleJava7 {

    public static void main(String[] args) {
        List<Book> books = getBooks();

        List<Book> programmingBooks = new ArrayList<>();
        for (Book book : books) {
            if (book.getType() == BookType.PROGRAMMING) {
                programmingBooks.add(book);
            }
        }
        Collections.sort(programmingBooks, new Comparator<Book>() {
            @Override
            public int compare(Book b1, Book b2) {
```

```
            return b1.getTitle().length() - b2.getTitle().length();
        }
    });
    for (Book book:  programmingBooks) {
        System.out.println(book.getTitle());
    }
  }
}
```

The code prints all the programming book titles, sorts them by their title length, and finally prints them to console. Java 7 developers write this kind of code every day. To write such a simple program, we had to write 15 lines of Java code. The bigger problem with the foregoing code is not the number of lines a developer has to write but the intent (i.e., filtering books, sorting by title length, and finally printing them).

We can simplify the foregoing code using the Java 8 stream API as shown in the following code:

```
public class ExampleJava8Stream {

    public static void main(String[] args) {
        List<Book> books = getBooks();

        List<String> programmingBookTitles = books.stream()
                .filter(book -> book.getType() == BookType.PROGRAMMING)
                .sorted((b1, b2) -> b1.getTitle().length() - b2.getTitle().length())
                .map(Book::getTitle)
                .collect(Collectors.toList());

        programmingBookTitles.forEach(System.out::println);
    }
}
```

The code constructs a pipeline comprising multiple stream operations, each discussed next.

- **stream()**: Created a stream pipeline by invoking the stream() method on the source collection (i.e., tasks List<Book>).

- **filter(Predicate<T>)**: This operation extracted elements in the stream matching the condition defined by the predicate. Once you have a stream you can call zero or more intermediate operations on it. The lambda expression book -> book.getType() == BookType.PROGRAMMING defined a predicate to filter all programming books. The type of lambda expression is java.util.function.Predicate<Book>.

- **sorted(Comparator<T>)**: This operation returns a stream consisting of all the stream elements sorted by the Comparator defined by lambda expression (i.e., (b1, b2) -> b1.getTitle().length() – b2.getTitle().length() in the example shown above).

- **map(Function<T,R>)**: This operation returns a stream after applying the Function<T,R> on each element of this stream.

- **collect(toList())**: This operation collects results of the operations performed on the stream into a List.

Optional<T>

Java 8 introduced a new data type, java.util.Optional<T>, which encapsulates an empty value. It makes the intent of the API clear. If a function returns a value of type Optional<T>, then it tells the clients that a value might not be present. Use of the Optional data type makes it explicit to the API client when it should expect an optional value. The purpose of using the Optional type is to help API designers make it visible to their clients, by looking at the method signature, whether or not they should expect an optional value. There are three creational methods that are part of the Optional API.

- **Optional.empty**: This is used to create an Optional when a value is not present. Rather than returning null, you return Optional.empty.

- **Optional.of(T value)**: This is used to create an Optional from a non-null value. It throws a NullPointerException when value is null. You will use it like Optional<String> mayBeName = Optional.of(name).

- **Optional.ofNullable(T value)**: This is a static factory method which works for both null and non-null values. For null value, it will create an empty Optional and for non-null value, it will create an Optional using the value.

Project Setup

This book follows a hands-on approach where we will learn TDD by working through an example. We will build an application **bookstoread** in this book. This application is similar to the www.goodreads.com/ web application. More functional details of the application will be covered in next chapter. This chapter will set up the project that you will use throughout this book. But before you can move ahead, we will have to do some setup. Please install the following on your machine:

- **Java 8**: JUnit 5 will work with Java 8 or above. Please download the latest update of Java 8 from the official oracle web site www. oracle.com/technetwork/java/javase/downloads/index.html. At the time of this writing, the Java version was 1.8.0_101. You can check your Java version by running the following command:

```
$ java -version
java version "1.8.0_101"
Java(TM) SE Runtime Environment (build 1.8.0_101-b13)
Java HotSpot(TM) 64-Bit Server VM (build 25.101-b13, mixed mode)
```

- **IntelliJ IDEA 2016.2 or above**: Many Java developers have moved from Eclipse to IntelliJ Idea IDE. We will be using latest community edition of IntelliJ. You can download the latest version from JetBrains web site www.jetbrains.com/idea/download/. IntelliJ Idea has good support for JUnit 5.

- **Gradle**: Gradle is a popular build tool in the JVM ecosystem. It is used for dependency management and running automated tasks. You don't need to install Gradle on your local machine. We will be using a Gradle wrapper that downloads and installs Gradle for your project. To learn more about Gradle you can refer to Gradle documentation https://docs.gradle.org/current/userguide/userguide.html.

Now, that we have all the prerequisites, let's create a Gradle project using IntelliJ Idea.

1. Launch the IntelliJ IDEA and you will see the following screen to create a project as shown in the Figure 1-3:

Figure 1-3. IntelliJ start

2. Click *Create New Project* to start the process of creating a Java Gradle project. You will see a screen to create a new project. Please select Gradle and Java as shown in Figure 1-4.

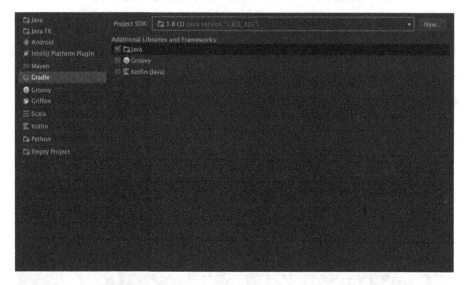

Figure 1-4. *Import project*

3. You will also have to specify the Project SDK. *Click* the *New* button to select JDK 8. Click Next to move to the next screen. Now, you will be asked to specify *GroupId* and *ArtifactId* as shown in Figure 1-5.

Figure 1-5. *Project properties*

4. Click the *Next* button to move the next screen. This screen will ask you to specify few Gradle settings. We will select Use *auto-import* so that Gradle automatically adds new dependencies when we add it to the build file. Also, we will select *Create directories for empty content roots automatically* option (refer to Figure 1-6).

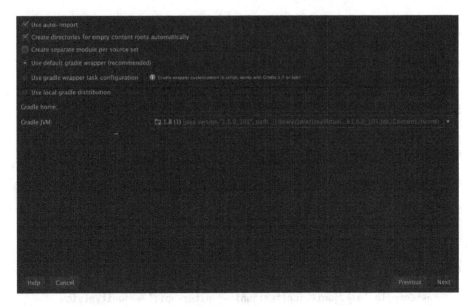

Figure 1-6. *Gradle properties*

5. Click the Next button to move to the final screen. In this
    screen, you will be asked the location where you want to
    create the project. Select a convenient directory path for the
    application. Finally, click the Finish button to complete the
    project creation process as shown in Figure 1-7.

Figure 1-7. *Project location*

We will cover JUnit 5 Gradle integration later in this book. So, for now just follow the steps related to Gradle.

Now, that our Java Gradle project is created we have to make a couple of changes in the Gradle build file (i.e., `build.gradle`). Open the `build.gradle` file in IDE and change it to match the following contents:

```
group 'com.junit5book'
version '1.0-SNAPSHOT'

apply plugin: 'java'

sourceCompatibility = 1.8

repositories {
    mavenCentral()
}

dependencies {
    def junitVersion = '5.0.1'
    testCompile 'org.junit.jupiter:junit-jupiter-api:' + junitVersion
    testCompile 'org.junit.jupiter:junit-jupiter-engine:' + junitVersion
}
```

In the `build.gradle` file showed in the code we have done the following:

- **Changed the sourceCompatibility from 1.5 to 1.8**: This property of the Gradle Java plug-in is used to specify which version of JVM to use. As we will be using JDK 1.8, we changed it to 1.8.

- **We added JUnit 5 dependencies in the dependencies section**: We need to add two dependencies–junit-jupiter-api and junit-jupiter-engine API. As discussed in section "JUnit 5," junit-jupiter-api defines the API that we need to write tests. The junit-jupiter-engine is the implementation of the junit-platform-engine API for JUnit 5.

That's all we need to do to start using JUnit 5. We will cover Gradle JUnit 5 integration in future chapters so refer to those chapters to learn more. In the next few chapters, we will run our test cases from within IDE.

Writing Your First Test

Let's start building the *bookstoread* application. The first functionality that we will support is the ability to add books to the BookShelf. In this chapter, we will not fully implement this functionality. We will just write enough code to test that when we create the bookshelf there are no books in it (i.e., it is empty).

We will start by writing a test specification. Create a new package bookstoread inside the src/main/test directory. We will keep flat package structures to make code easier to read. Inside the bookstoread package, we will create a new class BookShelfSpec.

If you have written JUnit test cases before then you would have normally written test classes that end with Test or Tests. In this book, we will follow the behavior-driven development (BDD) naming convention. The *Test naming convention forces you to think that your unit tests are the only quality assurance facility. We want you to think in terms of behavior specification so our tests will end with Spec.

You will have an empty specification class as shown in the code snippet.

```
package bookstoread;

public class BookShelfSpec {

}
```

Let's write our first test case, which will assert that when no book is added to the shelf it should be empty. Inside the BookShelfSpec, add test case that follows:

```
package bookstoread;

import org.junit.jupiter.api.Test;

import java.util.List;

import static org.junit.jupiter.api.Assertions.assertTrue;

public class BookShelfSpec {

    @Test
    public void shelfEmptyWhenNoBookAdded() throws Exception {
        BookShelf shelf = new BookShelf();
        List<String> books = shelf.books();
        assertTrue(books.isEmpty(), () -> "BookShelf should be empty.");
    }

}
```

The code will not compile, as there is no BookShelf class yet. At this point, we have just coded our client assuming that BookShelf will exist in future. We just want to get the feel of our API as a client. We have coded our expectation and how we want our API to look. As we learn more, we will refactor our API to meet our expectations.

A test case is broken down into the following three parts:

- We set up data that our test case needs.

- We call the unit being tested.

- We perform assertions to verify if expected behavior is correct.

This is also called AAA (Arrange, Act, and Assert).

In the test case just shown, you will notice that we have used org.unit.jupiter. api.Test annotation. In earlier versions of JUnit, the annotation was org.junit.Test. To write JUnit 5 test cases you have to use org.unit.jupiter.api.Test annotation. JUnit 5 distinguishes between different versions based on the annotation present on the test case.

JUnit 5 has trimmed down assertions support. There is no assertThat method in JUnit 5. It is expected that you will use a third-party assertion library like Hamcrest or AssertJ. We will use AssertJ in future chapters. In the code just shown, we have used the inbuilt assertion assertTrue, which tests whether the condition is true or not.

Let's write the code to make our test pass. Create a new class BookShelf in the src/main/java directory. Add books method to it as shown in Figure 1-8. This code will be generated if you use IntelliJ to create a class for you. To create BookShelf using IntelliJ, press alt + enter on the BookShelf in BookShelfSpec as shown in Figure 1-8.

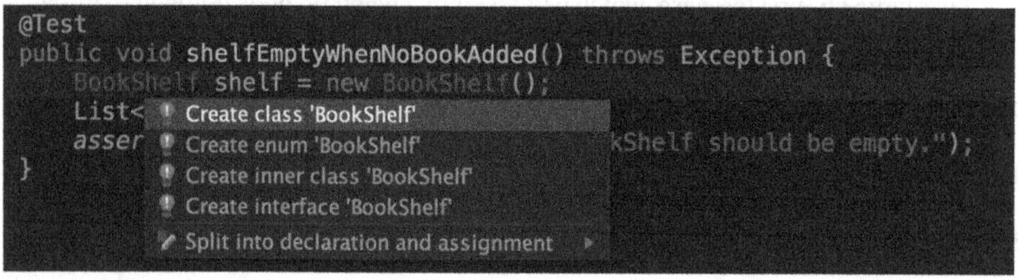

```
@Test
public void shelfEmptyWhenNoBookAdded() throws Exception {
    BookShelf shelf = new BookShelf();
    List<    Create class 'BookShelf'
    asser    Create enum 'BookShelf'                    kShelf should be empty.");
}           Create inner class 'BookShelf'
            Create interface 'BookShelf'
            Split into declaration and assignment  ▶
```

Figure 1-8. *Create class*

To create books method using IntelliJ shortcut again press alt + enter on the books method. Finally, you will have a class as shown in the code that follows:

```
package bookstoread;

import java.util.List;

public class BookShelf {

    public List<String> books() {
        return null;
    }
}
```

Now that our code compiles, let's run our test case. To run the test case, right-click the test class and select *Run 'BookShelfSpec'* as shown in Figure 1-9.

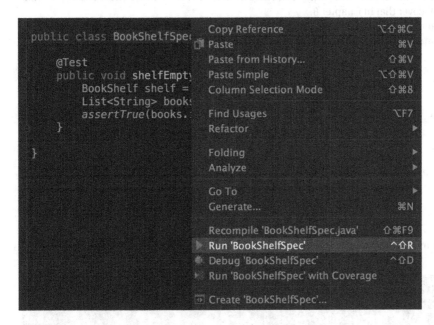

Figure 1-9. Run test

When you run the test, you will see test failure as shown in Figure 1-10.

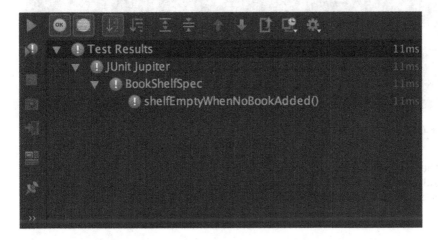

Figure 1-10. Test failure

One thing that you will notice in Figure 1-10 is a mention of JUnit Jupiter. Figure 1-10 shows that BookShelfSpec shelfEmptyWhenNoBookAdded test was executed by the JUnit Jupiter engine. If you have JUnit 4 test cases as well then you will see JUnit Vintage as well. We will cover that in Chapter 8.

To make this test case pass we will change the BookShelf books method implementation to return an empty list as shown in the code that follows:

```java
package bookstoread;

import java.util.Collections;
import java.util.List;

public class BookShelf {

    public List<String> books() {
        return Collections.emptyList();
    }
}
```

Run the test case again. This time you will see the happy green bar (see Figure 1-11).

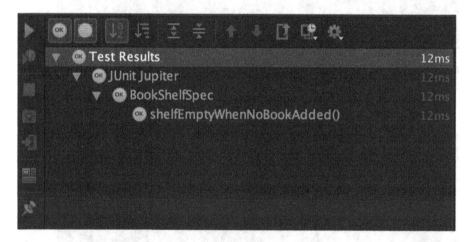

Figure 1-11. Test success

The green bar signifies that the code meets our expectations. We can now continue and add a new test case. We will continue this functionality in Chapter 3 after we have discussed the core concepts of JUnit 5.

Summary

In this chapter, you learned why developer testing is a valuable skill for every programmer. We covered TDD in detail and then talked about unit testing. Unit testing produces a necessary productivity boost for software developers by providing them a safety net against regressions and a guide that will help programmers design their applications.

This chapter also talked about JUnit, the de facto standard for unit testing in Java. JUnit 5 is a modular and extensibility version of JUnit. We concluded the chapter by creating a Java Gradle project using IntelliJ IDEA IDE and we wrote our first test case. In the next chapter, we will learn about the core concepts of JUnit 5.

CHAPTER 2

■ ■ ■

Understanding Core JUnit 5

In the first chapter, we learned the importance of test-driven development (TDD). We also discussed the pivotal role of unit testing. But before we move on to building an application using JUnit 5, it is important to understand its core concepts.

The goal of this chapter is to provide an overview of the core concepts of JUnit 5. JUnit 5 is founded on the following principles:

- Minimize footprint.

- Simplify test cases.

- Provide extensibility over features.

- Prefer specific plug points to general ones.

All these concepts make the new version focused on testing needs while being leaner and extensible. All in all, JUnit 5 is a complete rewrite of the JUnit framework, so a lot has changed underneath. Hence, even if you know the core concepts of previous versions of JUnit it is important that you understand how JUnit 5 differs.

Then, in the next chapter, we will start building a **bookstoread** application using JUnit 5. Building an application will help you learn how to apply these core concepts to your work.

Test Class

As a programmer, we interact with a unit-testing framework via test classes. In the first chapter, we wrote our first test class BookShelfSpec. It had one test method shelfEmptyWhenNoBookAdded, which asserted that BookShelf should be empty when no book is added to it.

In the previous versions of JUnit, a class is considered a test class if it has the following characteristics:

- Public access

- A no-arg constructor

- At least one test method

© Shekhar Gulati, Rahul Sharma 2017
S. Gulati, R. Sharma, *Java Unit Testing with JUnit 5*,
https://doi.org/10.1007/978-1-4842-3015-2_2

In the first chapter, we wrote the test class BookShelfSpec, shown in the following code, which satisfied those constraints:

```
package bookstoread;

import org.junit.jupiter.api.Test;
import java.util.List;
import static org.junit.jupiter.api.Assertions.assertTrue;

public class BookShelfSpec {

    @Test
    public void shelfEmptyWhenNoBookAdded() {
        BookShelf shelf = new BookShelf();
        List<String> books = shelf.books();
        assertTrue(books.isEmpty(), () -> "BookShelf should be empty");
    }

}
```

We do not have to write a no-arg constructor as Java creates one implicitly if a class does not have any other constructor.

In JUnit 5, a few of these constraints have been relaxed. JUnit 5 test classes and test methods are not required to be public. We can now make them package protected as shown in the code that follows:

```
// package and import statements removed for brevity

class BookShelfSpec {

    @Test
  void shelfEmptyWhenNoBookAdded(){
        BookShelf shelf = new BookShelf();
        List<String> books = shelf.books();
        assertTrue(books.isEmpty(), () -> "BookShelf should be empty.");
    }

}
```

The reason for this relaxation is that JUnit internally uses reflection to find test classes and test methods. Reflection can discover them even if they have limited visibility so there is no need for them to be public. It does not mean a lot, as test class and test method stubs can be easily generated using our favorite integrated development environment (IDE). So, as a programmer, we didn't have to do much previously as well. But, in my opinion, this is a subtle way to say that if you don't need something why ask for it. In this section, we will only focus on test classes. We cover test methods in the next section.

Constructors

JUnit 5 does not require a test class to have a public no-arg constructor. The constructor can be package protected, or protected, or even private. Following is the BookShelfSpec with the private no-arg constructor. Run the test case and you will see that the test still works fine.

```
class BookShelfSpec {
    private BookShelfSpec() {
        /*
        This constructor is private
        */
    }
    // test removed for brevity
}
```

The other constraint that prior versions of JUnit had on constructors was that they couldn't have parameters. We were required to have a public no-arg constructor. We saw that in JUnit 5 visibility constraint is relaxed, but does JUnit 5 also relax the no-arg constructor constraint? You would be pleasantly surprised that with JUnit 5 test class constructors are allowed to have parameters. Test methods can have not only constructors but also parameters. This is achieved by providing a ParameterResolver. A ParameterResolver dynamically resolves parameters at runtime. You can only use parameters in constructors or test methods if you have a resolver that will resolve these parameters and inject them. We will cover resolvers in more detail in a chapter 8. Just to give you a quick example, we will use one of the JUnit 5 inbuilt resolvers—TestInfoParameterResolver.

```
import org.junit.jupiter.api.TestInfo;

class BookShelfSpec {

    private BookShelfSpec(TestInfo testInfo) {
        System.out.println("Working on test " + testInfo.getDisplayName());
    }

    // test method removed for brevity

}
```

In the foregoing code, we defined a parameter of type TestInfo in the test class constructor that is later used in the print statement. TestInfoParameterResolver supplies an instance of TestInfo to the constructor. TestInfo contains information about the current test. We used it to display the name of the test class.

When you run, the code shown previously, it will print the statement "Working on test BookShelfSpec" for each test case. As we have just one test case, it will be printed only once.

Using @DisplayName

When they start working with JUnit, most programmers think that a test class name needs to end with Test suffix. Using Test in the test class name is just a convention; you are not required to name your test classes like that. These days many programmers end their test class names with Spec or Specification. So, rather than writing BookShelfTest we could write BookShelfSpec or BookShelfSpecification. The Spec naming convention is popularized by behavior-driven development (BDD) practice. Your goal should be to pick one naming convention and stick with it in your project.

Behavior-driven development combines TDD principles with domain-driven design to provide software teams with shared tools and a shared process to collaborate on software development.

JUnit 5 allows you to use custom names for your test classes. You can use org.junit.jupiter.api.DisplayName annotation to provide a name that can contain spaces, special characters, or even emoji. This allows you to use more meaningful names for your test classes. In the next chapter, we will use @DisplayName annotation for our test classes.

```java
import org.junit.jupiter.api.DisplayName;
import org.junit.jupiter.api.Test;
import org.junit.jupiter.api.TestInfo;

@DisplayName("<= BookShelf Specification =>")
class BookShelfSpec {

    private BookShelfSpec(TestInfo testInfo) {
        System.out.println("Working on test " + testInfo.getDisplayName());
    }

    @Test
    void shelfEmptyWhenNoBookAdded() {
      // removed for brevity
    }

}
```

When you run the BookShelfSpec in your IDE, you will see BookShelf Specification as the name of the test class being executed as shown in Figure 2-1.

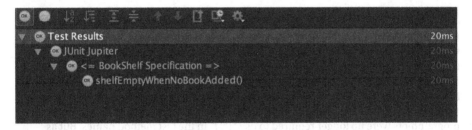

Figure 2-1. Test success

Test Method

In previous versions of JUnit, a test method exhibited the following characteristics:

- Should be annotated with org.junt.Test annotation.

- Should have public visibility.

- Should not take any arguments.

- Should return void.

In the previous section, we discussed that test methods are no longer required to be public in JUnit 5. A test method can be either protected or package protected. The preferred is to use package protected as that leads to less typing.

Tests in JUnit 5 must be annotated with org.junit.jupiter.api.Test annotation. This is different from the annotation used in JUnit 4. JUnit 5 designers went with a different annotation so that they could differentiate between different versions of JUnit. JUnit 5 can run both JUnit 4 and JUnit 5 tests based on which @Test annotation is used.

Parameters in Test Methods

As with test class constructors, test methods can also take parameters in JUnit 5. The code that follows is an example of a test method takes TestInfo as its parameter:

```
@Test
void shelfEmptyWhenNoBookAdded(TestInfo testInfo) {
    System.out.println("Working on test case " + testInfo.getDisplayName());
    BookShelf shelf = new BookShelf();
    List<String> books = shelf.books();
    assertTrue(books.isEmpty(), () -> "BookShelf should be empty.");
}
```

The foregoing code makes use of the ParameterResolver API (application programming interface) of JUnit 5. We will learn more about it later in this book.

Using @DisplayName

It is said that the most difficult problem in programming is naming. Most programmers find it difficult to give good names to classes, methods, and variables. This is true for test methods also. We have seen test methods with the names test1, test2, testSomeMethodName, and so on. The root cause of "test" in the name of the test methods is that JUnit versions prior to version 4 required test method names to start with "test" so that JUnit could find test methods. After the introduction of @Test annotation in JUnit 4, programmers were no longer required to use "test" in the test method names. But as people say, "old habits die hard," so most programmers stuck with the older convention.

Many TDD gurus and evangelists have raised test name concerns at various conferences and meetups. They have been urging people to start using better names for their test cases.

> *Test names should tell what behavior they are testing rather than names of the methods they are testing.*
>
> — Steve Freeman, Agile guru

Most programmers think a test method name has a one-to-one correspondence between a test method and a production class method. This is not true. We usually end up writing more than one behavior test for a single method.

Test method names must express their intent. We gave a behavioral name, shelfEmptyWhenNoBookAdded, to our test method. If someone reads the test name, he/she will know what behavior we are testing. But the problem with using behavior as a method name is that it leads to very long method names. Also, we can't use spaces in method names so readability suffers.

> *Test names which are written as short declarative statements are much more expressive than names which are machine readable i.e. they only make sense if you have an understanding of a hidden code language to dissect their meaning.*
>
> — Roy Osherove, author of *The Art of Unit Testing*

In programming languages like Groovy, we can use String as test names, which mean we can use spaces in method names. In Java, there are strict rules for method naming so programmers often use an underscore (_), as shown in the code that follows, which makes it more readable:

```
@Test
void shelf_empty_when_no_book_added() {
    BookShelf shelf = new BookShelf();
    List<String> books = shelf.books();
    assertTrue(books.isEmpty(), () -> "BookShelf should be empty.");
}
```

The @DisplayName annotation that we discussed in the previous section is used with test methods to provide meaningful names, as shown in the code that follows:

```
@DisplayName("A bookshelf")
class BookShelfSpec {

    @Test
    @DisplayName("is empty when no book is added to it")
    void shelfEmptyWhenNoBookAdded() {
        BookShelf shelf = new BookShelf();
        List<String> books = shelf.books();
        assertTrue(books.isEmpty(), () -> "BookShelf should be empty.");
    }

}
```

In the BookShelfSpec class shown previously, we used @DisplayName annotation with both the test class and the test method to provide readable names. Run the test again and you will see a more readable test output as shown in Figure 2-2.

Figure 2-2. Test case execution with @DisplayName annotation

Assertions

Assertions in JUnit are static methods that we call in our test methods to verify expected behavior. Each assertion tests whether the given condition is true or not. If an asserted condition does not evaluate to true then a test failure is reported. All JUnit 5 assertions are defined as part of org.junit.jupiter.api.Assertions class. In the single test case that we have written so far, we used assertTrue.

As mentioned in Chapter 1, there are fewer assertions in JUnit 5 compared to JUnit 4. In future chapters, we will use AssertJ, a third-party library that helps in writing clean assertions. For now, let's learn what comes inbuilt with JUnit 5.

JUnit 4 supported two assertion syntaxes–traditional assertions that shipped with original version of JUnit like `assertTrue`, `assertEquals`, etc., and a more readable syntax with `assertThat`. JUnit 5 does not support `assertThat` syntax. It is expected that you will use third-party libraries like AssertJ or Hamcrest to write `assertThat` assertions.

Each `assertXXX` method provided by JUnit has at least three overloaded methods. Let's look at one of the assertion methods `assertNull`. Following is a test case that makes use of all the overloaded `assertNull` methods:

```
@Test
void nullAssertionTest() {
    String str = null;
    assertNull(str);
    assertNull(str, "str should be null");
    assertNull(str, () -> "str should be null");
}
```

- In this case, the first `assertNull` checks that the value (i.e., str) is null. If the value is not null then `AssertionFailedError` will be thrown and the test will fail.

- The second overloaded method allows you to pass in a String message that will be shown to the user when a test fails. It's a best practice to provide an error message for all your assertion method calls.

- The third method makes use of Java 8 `java.util.function.Supplier` functional interface. We passed it a lambda expression that will generate the required message. The advantage of this method is that failure message will be retrieved lazily from the supplier only when an assertion fails. In case you are building a complex message, then, by using a supplier, you will only pay the cost if failure happens.

Assert methods with two value parameters follow a pattern. The first parameter is the expected value and second parameter is the actual value.

Table 2-1 lists some of the most popular assert methods that exist in JUnit 5.

Table 2-1. *Assertions*

Assert Method	What It Does
assertTrue	Assert that condition is true
assertFalse	Assert that condition is false
assertNull	Assert that object is null
assertNotNull	Assert that object is not null
assertEquals	Assert that expected and actual are equal
assertNotEquals	Assert that expected and actual are not equal
assertArrayEquals	Assert that expected and actual arrays are equals
assertSame	Assert that expected and actual refer to the same object
assertNotSame	Assert that expected and actual do not refer to the same object

It is important to note that assertTrue and assertFalse have one more overloaded method, besides the previously discussed three variants. It takes a java.util.function. BooleanSupplier as an argument. The method could be passed a lambda expression or we could combine it with stream, predicates, and partial functions to completely express our expectations.

```
@Test
void shouldCheckForEvenNumbers() {
  int number = new Random(10).nextInt();
  assertTrue(() -> number%2 == 0, number+ " is not an even number.");

  BiFunction<Integer, Integer, Boolean> divisible = (x, y) -> x % y == 0;
  Function<Integer, Boolean> multipleOf2 = (x) -> divisible.apply(x, 2);
  assertTrue(() -> multipleOf2.apply(number), () -> " 2 is not factor of " +
  number);

  List<Integer> numbers = Arrays.asList(1, 1, 1, 1, 2);
  assertTrue(() -> numbers.stream().distinct().anyMatch(DSLTest::isEven),
  "Did not find an even number in the list");
}

static boolean isEven(int number) {
  return number % 2 == 0;
}
```

In the foregoing test case, we are using a couple of things.

- The first assertion shows how a simple lambda expression can be used.

- In the next assertion, we built a couple of functions (e.g., divisible and multipleof2) and used them to test divisibility by 2.

- In the last assertion, we used a stream of integers along with a predicate to know if it contains an even number or not.

Another thing to note here is that JUnit 5 changed the order of message parameter. In JUnit 4, the message used to be the first argument, but in JUnit 5 message it is the last argument.

Table 2-2. *JUnit 4 vs. JUnit 5 assert method Parameter List*

JUnit 4	JUnit 5
assert*(message, expected, actual)	assert*(expected, actual, message)

JUnit 5 also has a fail method, which existed in previous versions of JUnit as well. It is used to fail a test with the given failure message. It also has an overloaded variant that takes a supplier.

```
@Test
void thisTestShouldFail() {
    fail(() -> "This test should fail");
}
```

Unlike JUnit 4, JUnit 5 provides the following methods for asserting exceptions:

- assertThrows(Class<? extends Throwable> expectedType, Executable executable): This assertion asserts that the supplied executable throws an exception of the type expectedType. This is a new way to assert exception in JUnit 5. You don't need the exception rules of JUnit 4 to test exceptions. We will cover this method in chapter 5.

Grouping Assertions

JUnit is designed to work best with a number of small tests. It executes each test within a separate instance of the test class. It reports failure on each test. Shared setup code is most natural when sharing between tests. This is a design decision that permeates JUnit, and when you decide to report multiple failures per test, you begin to fight against JUnit. This is not recommended.

FAQ, JUnit 4.0

JUnit advocates the practice of having a single assertion per test. When we say single assertion, it means testing a single behavior. The test written in the previous code shouldCheckForEvenNumbers is a violation of the proposed concept as here we are testing three different things.

But still, if we are testing a single unit we could be asserting a couple of properties (e.g., a test for toString method of BookShelf).

```
@Test
  public void shelfToStringShouldPrintBookCountAndTitles() throws Exception {
    BookShelf shelf = new BookShelf();
    List<String> books = shelf.books();
    shelf.add("The Phoenix Project");
    shelf.add("Java 8 in Action");
    String shelfStr = shelf.toString();
    assertTrue(shelfStr.contains("The Phoenix Project"),  "1st book title
    missing");
    assertTrue(shelfStr.contains("Java 8 in Action") , "2nd book title
    missing ");
    assertTrue(shelfStr.contains("2 books found"), "Book  count missing");
  }
```

The foregoing test case will break on the first assertion. But this may not represent the correct information. We would like to run all asserts to see the complete test result as shown in Figure 2-3.

Figure 2-3. *Test failure without group assertion*

The assertAll comes to our rescue. The assertion can be used to club all related assertions and run them as a single assertion to report only the failed ones. Each of the assertions is specified as a lambda expression.

```
@Test
  public void shelfToStringShouldPrintBookCountAndTitles() throws Exception {
      BookShelf shelf = new BookShelf();
      List<String> books = shelf.books();
      shelf.add("The Phoenix Project");
      shelf.add("Java 8 in Action");
      String shelfStr = shelf.toString();
      assertAll( ()  -> assertTrue(shelfStr.contains("The Phoenix
      Project"),  "1st book title missing"),
```

```
            () -> assertTrue(shelfStr.contains("Java 8 in Action") ,
            "2nd book title missing "),
            () -> assertTrue(shelfStr.contains("2 books found"),
            "Book  count missing"));
    }
```

Now in case of a failure we would have the following output. It lists all of the individual failed assertions as shown in Figure 2-4.

Optionally we could we also pass a string as the first argument. The string will be used as heading for all the failed exceptions.

Figure 2-4. *assertAll failure output*

Error vs. Failure

In JUnit, there is a difference between error and failure. A test fails when an assertion is not met and an error occurs when your test throws an unexpected exception. Let's assume we have the following example test class, which has two test methods:

```java
import org.junit.jupiter.api.Test;

import static org.junit.jupiter.api.Assertions.assertFalse;
import static org.junit.jupiter.api.Assertions.assertTrue;

class FailureAndErrorTests {

    @Test
    void stringIsNotEmpty() {
        String str = "";
        assertFalse(str.isEmpty());
    }

    @Test
    void thisMethodThrowsException() {
        String str = null;
```

```
        assertTrue(str.isEmpty());
    }
}
```

If you run the foregoing code, `stringIsNotEmpty` will be reported as failure whereas `thisMethodThrowsException` will be reported as an error. In tools like IntelliJ Idea, failures are shown in orange whereas errors are shown in red as you can see in Figure 2-5.

Figure 2-5. *Test error and failure*

JUnit Life Cycle API

A typical JUnit test class has multiple test cases. Each of the test cases is governed by a test life cycle. The complete cycle consists of the following three phases:

1. The first is the setup phase, where the test infrastructure is put in place. JUnit provides two levels of setup. One is the class level where a costly object like database connection can be created which can be reused for all the tests without any side effect. Test objects affecting test runs need to be created in the individual test setup methods.

2. The next is the test execution itself. Result verification is also part of the test execution phase. The execution result will signify a success or failure.

3. The last phase is the cleanup phase where any cleanup required after posttest execution is performed. Just like the class-level setup, there is a class-level cleanup also, which can be used to dispose of all the singletons created at the class level.

The JUnit API provides the annotations to perform test case setup and cleanup (see Figure 2-6).

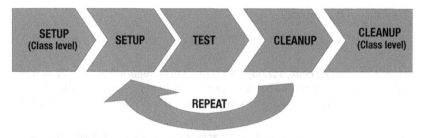

Figure 2-6. *Test life cycle*

@BeforeAll

The org.junit.jupiter.api.BeforeAll annotation is responsible for performing a single time initialization for all test cases in a class. The method must be static and non-private. It is often used to create costly objects like database connection, which can be reused for all the test cases. The work done in a BeforeAll can be moved to BeforeEach, but since it is usually a computationally expensive operation, the overall test execution can take much longer.

The annotation also has an inherited behavior. If there are superclass methods marked with @BeforeAll they will be executed before any such methods of the test class.

@BeforeEach

The org.junit.jupiter.api.BeforeEach annotation is responsible for performing any initialization before executing a single test. The objects will be created for each test, thus doing away with any side effects from other test executions.

It is a good idea to keep tests independent. If tests are dependent then a complete test suite becomes very hard to read and understand. Also in the event of a failure tests become very hard to debug. Imagine a case of testA dependent on testB that depends on testC. Now if testA fails we need to expend effort to determine if all of the previous test cases executed fine and properly initialized the test setup. This is unwanted Test Smell.

A test case can have any number of methods marked with BeforeEach but the execution order is not guaranteed. The JUnit engine can run them in any order. These methods are executed before each and every test; so always make sure they contain initialization code that makes sense for all test cases.

The annotation also has an inherited behavior. If there are superclass methods or interface default methods marked with @BeforeEach, they will be executed before any such methods of the test class.

@AfterEach

The org.junit.jupiter.api.AfterEach annotation is the counterpart of the org.junit.jupiter.api.BeforeEach annotation. It is used to implement the "what goes up must come down" principle. A method marked with @AfterEach is responsible for posttest execution cleanup. The method must be static and non-private. The annotation also has an inherited behavior. If there are superclass methods or interface default methods marked with @AfterEach, they will be executed after any such methods of the test class.

@AfterAll

The org.junit.jupiter.api.AfterAll annotation is the counterpart of the org.junit.jupiter.api.BeforeAll annotation. AfterAll performs a single time method invocation (i.e., post the execution of all test cases of a test class). The method must be static and non-private. The annotation also has an inherited behavior. If there are superclass methods marked with @AfterAll they will be executed after any such methods of the test class.

In our current user story, we have used only @BeforeEach but let's say tomorrow we build a BookShelf backed by a database. Then we could use all these annotations in the following manner:

```
class BookShelf Spec {
    @BeforeAll
    static void connectDBConnectionPool() {
    }

    @BeforeEach
    void initializeBookShelf WithDatabase() {
    }

    @Test
    void shouldGiveBackAllBooksInShelf() {
            // Check books in shelf
    }

    @AfterEach
    void deleteShelfFromDB() {
    }

    @AfterAll
    static void closeDBConnectionPool() {
    }

}
```

Optionally, we could extract out the @BeforeAll and @AfterAll methods to a superclass. This would clean up the duplicate code if the database is being used in more test cases.

```
abstract class DBConnectionPool{
        @BeforeAll
        static void connectDBConnectionPool() {
        }

        @AfterAll
        static void closeDBConnectionPool() {
        }

}
class BookShelf Spec extends DBConnectionPool{
        @BeforeEach
        void initializeShelfWithDatabase() {
        }

        @Test
        void shouldGiveBackAllBooksInShelf() {
                // Check books in shelf
        }

        @AfterEach
        void deleteCartFromDB() {
        }
}
```

The JUnit test execution engine builds an instance of the test class for each test method. This helps to keep test execution independent and removes the impact of one test on other tests. This per-test instance behavior enforces to build static methods for @BeforeAll and @AfterAll. The per-test instance can be changed to single instance for all tests. In order to do so annotate the class with @TestListener(Lifecycle.PER_CLASS). As a result the JUnit test execution will create a single instance. It will no longer ask to make @BeforeAll/@afterAll methods static. In such a scenario one test execution can influence other test executions, as testcase state is shared across all tests. Thus, any such variables must be cleared explicitly in @BeforeEach/@AfterEach methods.

Test Execution

In this section, we will learn how tests are discovered and executed. JUnit 5 is divided into various modules that we discussed in Chapter 1. Two of the modules that will help us understand how test discovery and execution happens are junit-platform-launcher and junit-platform-engine. junit-platform-launcher defines the API that is used by tools like IDE to discover and execute tests. junit-platform-engine provides an API that we can use to write our own test engine. The test engine that we have been using so far is junit-jupiter-engine. Let's look at all the steps that are executed behind the scenes to run your test cases.

1. It all starts by creating an instance of org.junit.platform. launcher.Launcher. Launcher API is the entry point that tools like IDE use to discover and execute tests. Test execution does not happen in launcher. A launcher detects supported test engines and engines do the execution of tests. JUnit 5 provides a default implementation of Launcher org.junit.platform. launcher.core.DefaultLauncher that you can create using the org.junit.platform.launcher.core.LauncherFactory. DefaultLauncher is package protected so you can't create its instance directly. You have to use LauncherFactory to create an instance. You can write your own Launcher by implementing Launcher API, but most of the time it will not be required.

2. To use Launcher API, you have to add it to your class path. In your build file, add the following to the dependencies section.

    ```
    testCompile 'org.junit.platform:junit-platform-launcher: 1.0.1'
    ```

3. Once you have added the dependency, you can create a new instance of Launcher as shown in the following code:

    ```java
    import org.junit.platform.launcher.Launcher;
    import org.junit.platform.launcher.core.LauncherFactory;

    public class TestLauncher {

        public static void main(String[] args) {
            Launcher launcher = LauncherFactory.create();
        }
    }
    ```

CHAPTER 2 ■ UNDERSTANDING CORE JUNIT 5

4. The LauncherFactory.create method creates an instance
    of DefaultLauncher. The DefaultLauncher constructor
    takes an Iterable of TestEngine. As discussed before, JUnit
    supports a TestEngine API, which is defined in module
    junit-platform-engine. There are currently two TestEngine
    implementations defined in junit-jupiter-engine (for
    JUnit 5) and junit-vintage-engine (for JUnit 4 and below).
    To discover the TestEngine implementations, JUnit 5 relies
    on JDK java.util.ServiceLoader facility. JDK 6 introduced the
    concept of ServiceLoader that allowed developers to extend
    their code with new functionality by adding a new JAR onto
    the application class path. In the Service Loader pattern, all
    implementations are discovered using a file in the META-INF/
    services directory. If you look inside the junit-jupiter-
    engine module, you will find that there is a file named org.
    junit.platform.engine.TestEngine inside the META-INF/
    services directory. It contains one entry, the implementation
    of org.junit.platform.engine.TestEngine.

    ```
    org.junit.jupiter.engine.JupiterTestEngine
    ```

5. The code that follows is executed by JUnit 5 to discover all the
    TestEngine's present on the class path:

    ```
    Iterable<TestEngine> testEngines = ServiceLoader.load(TestEngine.
    class,ReflectionUtils.getDefaultClassLoader());
    ```

6. Once the test engines are discovered, listeners
    are registered with the Launcher by calling the
    registerTestExecutionListeners method on them.
    The type of listener is org.junit.platform.launcher.
    TestExecutionListener. There are few implementations
    provided by JUnit 5 itself. We will register the JUnit 5
    provided TestExecutionListener org.junit.platform.
    launcher.listeners.SummaryGeneratingListener.
    SummaryGeneratingListener generates the summary of test
    execution. Let's modify our TestLauncher to register a listener
    as shown in the code that follows:

    ```
    import org.junit.platform.launcher.Launcher;
    import org.junit.platform.launcher.core.LauncherFactory;
    import org.junit.platform.launcher.listeners.
    SummaryGeneratingListener;
    public class TestLauncher {
        public static void main(String[] args) {
            Launcher launcher = LauncherFactory.create();
    ```

```
SummaryGeneratingListener summaryGeneratingListener = new
SummaryGeneratingListener();
launcher.registerTestExecutionListeners(summaryGenerating
Listener);
    }
}
```

7. We can register more than one listener with a launcher as the registerTestExecutionListeners method takes a vararg of TestExecutionListener.

8. The next step is to send the discovery request to a registered TestEngine. To do that, we first create a new org.junit. platform.launcher.LauncherDiscoveryRequest using the org.junit.platform.launcher.core.LauncherDiscoveryRe questBuilder as shown in the code. In the following code, we are telling our request that it should find all the tests inside the booktoread package.

```
LauncherDiscoveryRequest discoveryRequest =
                LauncherDiscoveryRequestBuilder
                        .request()
                        .selectors(DiscoverySelectors.
                        selectPackage("bookstoread"))
                        .build();
We send the request to registered engines using the execute method.
launcher.execute(discoveryRequest);
```

9. The execute method executes a TestPlan which is built according to the supplied LauncherDiscoveryRequest by querying all the registered engines and collecting their results. The registered listeners are notified of the progress and execution results. To view the summary of our test results we can call the getSummary method of SummaryGeneratingListener as shown in the following code:

```
import org.junit.platform.engine.discovery.DiscoverySelectors;
import org.junit.platform.launcher.Launcher;
import org.junit.platform.launcher.LauncherDiscoveryRequest;
import org.junit.platform.launcher.core.
LauncherDiscoveryRequestBuilder;
import org.junit.platform.launcher.core.LauncherFactory;
import org.junit.platform.launcher.listeners.
SummaryGeneratingListener;
import java.io.PrintWriter;
public class TestLauncher {
    public static void main(String[] args) {
        Launcher launcher = LauncherFactory.create();
```

```
            SummaryGeneratingListener summaryGeneratingListener = new
            SummaryGeneratingListener();
            launcher.registerTestExecutionListeners(summaryGenerating
            Listener);
            LauncherDiscoveryRequest discoveryRequest =
                    LauncherDiscoveryRequestBuilder
                            .request()
                            .selectors(DiscoverySelectors.
                            selectPackage("bookstoread"))
                            .build();
            launcher.execute(discoveryRequest);
            summaryGeneratingListener.getSummary().printTo(new
            PrintWriter(System.out));
        }
    }
```

10. If you run the TestLauncher shown previously, you will see following output:

```
Test run finished after 53 ms
[           1 tests found      ]
[           0 tests skipped    ]
[           1 tests started    ]
[           0 tests aborted    ]
[           1 tests successful ]
[           0 tests failed     ]
[           0 containers failed]
```

The test output clearly shows that we executed one test and it was successful. TestEngine creates a new instance of the test class before invoking each test method. This helps to make tests independent, as you can't rely on their execution order, hence avoiding any unintentional side effect.

Summary

In this chapter, you learned the core concepts of JUnit 5 and how JUnit 5 is different from previous versions of JUnit. You learned how JUnit 5 relaxes some of the constraints on test classes and methods, leading to clean tests. You also learned how you could provide human-readable names to your test classes and methods using the @DisplayName annotation.

We ended the chapter with coverage on how tests are discovered and executed using the Launcher and TestEngine APIs. In the next chapter, we will start working on the bookstoread application following TDD practice and making use of JUnit 5 features.

■ ■ ■

CHAPTER 3

Developing an Application with JUnit 5

In the previous chapter, we learned about JUnit 5 fundamentals and how JUnit 5 executes tests. We learned about JUnit 5 core classes and methods, and how they interact with each other. Now, we have a solid base to start building the bookstoread application.

In this chapter, we will go real and build few features of the application we started in previous chapters. We will build features iteratively following test-driven development (TDD) practice. This will help you master the TDD continuous cycle of RED ➤ GREEN ➤ REFACTOR that we discussed previously.

In the process of writing the application, you will learn and master new features of JUnit 5.

Bookstoread Application

Bookstoread is a social cataloging web site that allows users to create virtual bookshelves where they can add the books they want to read. They will be able to arrange their bookshelves based on different criteria (author name, book title, publication year, etc.). Also, they will be able to mark reading progress and see how well they are doing.

In this section we are going to build features of the application.

First Feature

As a user, I want to add multiple books to my bookshelf so that I can read them later.

© Shekhar Gulati, Rahul Sharma 2017
S. Gulati, R. Sharma, *Java Unit Testing with JUnit 5*,
https://doi.org/10.1007/978-1-4842-3015-2_3

Write a Failing Test

We will start by developing our first feature, adding multiple books to the bookshelf. In the first chapter, we wrote our first test case for this use case as shown in the following code:

```
@Test
public void emptyBookShelfWhenNoBookAdded() {
    BookShelf shelf = new BookShelf();
    List<String> books = shelf.books();
    assertTrue(books.isEmpty(), () -> "BookShelf should be empty.");
}
```

To make this test case pass, we wrote just enough code to make it pass.

```
import java.util.Collections;
import java.util.List;

public class BookShelf {

    public List<String> books() {
        return Collections.emptyList();
    }
}
```

Let's write our second test case, which will verify that if we add two books to the shelf, the bookshelf will have two books. We will keep things simple and use String to denote books. We will delay the decision to have a domain object for the book until the appropriate time. Our tests will help us decide when we should have a proper type for books.

```
@Test
void bookshelfContainsTwoBooksWhenTwoBooksAdded() {
    BookShelf shelf = new BookShelf();
    shelf.add("Effective Java");
    shelf.add("Code Complete");
    List<String> books = shelf.books();
    assertEquals(2, books.size(), () -> "BookShelf should have two books.");
}
```

In the foregoing code, we wrote a test case that adds two books to the shelf by calling the add method twice on the BookShelf object. After adding books, we called the books method on the BookShelf and asserted that it contains two books.

This test case will not compile right now as we have not yet defined the add method in the BookShelf. Create the add method in the BookShelf class as shown in the following code so that the code compiles:

```
public void add(String bookToAdd) {
}
```

The foregoing addition to the BookShelf class will make our code compile. Run all the tests again; this time the bookshelfContainsTwoBooksWhenTwoBooksAdded test case will fail as shown in Figure 3-1. In Figure 3-1, we can see that our previous test case still works.

Figure 3-1. Failed test

Each time, run all the test cases to make sure all the previous tests are green. As you add more tests, it is very important to make sure previous test cases are working well.

Make Test Pass

Let's make the test case pass by writing the following code:

```
package bookstoread;

import java.util.ArrayList;
import java.util.List;

public class BookShelf {

    private final List<String> books = new ArrayList<>();

    public List<String> books() {
        return books;
    }

    public void add(String bookToAdd) {
        books.add(bookToAdd);
    }
}
```

In the foregoing code, we did following:

1. We created an instance variable books of the type List<String> to store books.

2. We changed the books method to return the books instance variable.

3. We implemented the add method by adding bookToAdd to the books list.

Run the test case and this time the test will pass (see Figure 3-2).

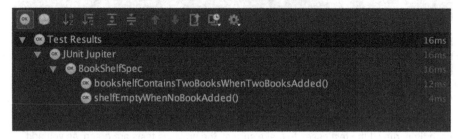

Figure 3-2. *Test success*

Refactor the Code

Now that we have two passing tests, let's see if we have something to refactor. One thing that we can improve is allowing the user to add multiple books at once. We can refactor the add method to take a vararg method argument instead of simple String. Let's make this change.

```
public void add(String... booksToAdd) {
    Arrays.stream(booksToAdd).forEach(book -> books.add(book));
}
```

In the foregoing code, we first used the Java 8 Arrays.stream method to convert booksToAdd to a Stream<String> and then used the forEach method on the Stream to add each book to the books collection.

We can use Java 8 method references to make the add method terser as shown in Figure 3-3.

```
public void add(String... booksToAdd) {
    Arrays.stream(booksToAdd).forEach(book -> books.add(book));
}
```
```
● Replace lambda with method reference    ▶
  Go to super method                     ⌘U
  Expand lambda expression body to {...}  ▶
```

Figure 3-3. *Replace lambda with method reference*

```
public void add(String... booksToAdd) {
    Arrays.stream(booksToAdd).forEach(books::add);
}
```

If you are using IntelliJ then you can use the shortcut ALT+Enter to convert a lambda expression to method reference as shown below.

Run your test cases again to verify that all tests are still green. Refactoring should never change the behavior of the program, so tests written against expected behavior should remain green. If you write tests that depend on the internal state of the program then there is a good chance that they might stop working after refactoring. This is the reason we recommend that you write tests against public API (application programming interface) methods and your tests should document expected behavior, not implementation.

We changed the add method signature to make it easy for BookShelf clients to add multiple books in one method call. As the test case is the first client of your code, it will tell you if you can improve the API. Let's refactor our test case to pass multiple books in one method call.

```
@Test
public void bookshelfContainsTwoBooksWhenTwoBooksAdded() {
    BookShelf shelf = new BookShelf();
    shelf.add("Effective Java", "Code Complete");
    List<String> books = shelf.books();
    assertEquals(2, books.size(), () -> "BookShelf should have two books.");
}
```

Run the test again and all tests should still be green.

Add Test Cases for Exception Scenarios

There is nothing more to refactor so let's move to the next test case. Do we need to write a new test case? If you read the user story again you will find that we have achieved the functionality that we intended to write in this user story. But we can still write a few more behavioral tests to be sure what will happen in exceptional situations.

Let's write a test case that tests the scenario where we call the add method without passing any book. We expect that we should get an empty bookshelf as shown in the code that follows:

```
@Test
public void emptyBookShelfWhenAddIsCalledWithoutBooks() {
    BookShelf shelf = new BookShelf();
    shelf.add();
    List<String> books = shelf.books();
    assertTrue(books.isEmpty(), () -> "BookShelf should be empty.");
}
```

Run the tests to verify that all tests still pass. You will find all tests are green. Now, we are sure that nothing will go wrong if we call the add method without any parameters.

One last test case that we can add for this user story is to make sure that the client of BookShelf can't modify the books collection returned by the books method.

```
@Test
void booksReturnedFromBookShelfIsImmutableForClient() {
    BookShelf shelf = new BookShelf();
    shelf.add("Effective Java", "Code Complete");
    List<String> books = shelf.books();
    try {
        books.add("The Mythical Man-Month");
        fail(() -> "Should not be able to add book to books");
    } catch (Exception e) {
        assertTrue(e instanceof UnsupportedOperationException, () -> "Should
        throw UnsupportedOperationException.");
    }
}
```

In the foregoing test case, we first added a couple of books to the shelf and then tried to add another book (which we got by calling the books method of BookShelf) to the books collection. We expected that adding a book to the books collection would throw an UnsupportedOperationException. If no exception is thrown then we fail the test by calling the JUnit's fail method. We will cover how to test exceptions in detail in Chapter 5. JUnit 5 has substantially improved the way you can write tests for exceptions. So, stay tuned!

Run all the test cases again. Our new test case will fail, as the collection that we received from the books method is mutable so we were able to successfully add a book to it.

To make the test pass, we will change the books method to return an immutable list as shown in the code snippet that follows:

```
public List<String> books() {
    return Collections.unmodifiableList(books);
}
```

Run the test again and all tests should be green.

Using @BeforeEach

If we look at the test case, the test initialization is being duplicated for each test. We can extract the code to a method and annotate it with @BeforeEach.

```
public class BookShelfSpec {

    private BookShelf shelf;

    @BeforeEach
    void init() throws Exception {
        shelf = new BookShelf();
    }

    @Test
    public void emptyBookShelfWhenNoBookAdded() {
        List<String> books = shelf.books();
        assertTrue(books.isEmpty(), () -> "BookShelf should be empty.");
    }

    @Test
    void bookshelfContainsTwoBooksWhenTwoBooksAdded() {
        shelf.add("Effective Java", "Code Complete");
        List<String> books = shelf.books();
        assertEquals(2, books.size(), () -> "BookShelf should have two books.");
    }

    // Rest code removed for brevity

}
```

Run all the tests again to verify that they are still green. Now that the code is in good shape, we can start working on the next feature.

Second Feature

As a user, I should be able to arrange my bookshelf based on certain criteria

Write a Failing Test Case

The next feature helps the user to arrange the bookshelf based on certain criteria. The criteria can be the book name, the author name, the book publication date, or a combination of all.

Let us start on this feature by arranging books lexicographically by their title.

```
@Test
void bookshelfArrangedByBookTitle() {
    BookShelf shelf = new BookShelf();
    shelf.add("Effective Java", "Code Complete","The Mythical Man-Month" );
    List<String> books = shelf.arrange();
    assertEquals(Arrays.asList( "Code Complete", "Effective Java", "The
    Mythical Man-Month"), books, () -> "Books in a bookshelf should be
    arranged lexicographically by book title");
}
```

The foregoing code will not compile as the arrange method is not defined. To make the code compile, let's add the arrange method to the BookShelf.

```
public List<String> arrange() {
    return null;
}
```

Run all the test cases and you will find that our new test case fails.

Make Test Pass

To make our test case pass we will have to return a sorted books collection.

```
public List<String> arrange() {
    books.sort(Comparator.naturalOrder());
    return books;
}
```

Run the test case and everything will be green.

Did you notice a problem with the foregoing implementation? We are sorting the underlying collection, which means if we call the books method after arranging it will also return a sorted collection. We would like to keep the insertion order for the books method. Let's write a test case for that.

```
@Test
void booksInBookShelfAreInInsertionOrderAfterCallingArrange() {
    BookShelf shelf = new BookShelf();
    shelf.add("Effective Java", "Code Complete", "The Mythical Man-Month");
    shelf.arrange();
    List<String> books = shelf.books();
    assertEquals(Arrays.asList("Effective Java", "Code Complete", "The Mythical
    Man-Month"), books, () -> "Books in bookshelf are in insertion order");
}
```

This test case will fail. To fix this, we must return a new sorted collection.

```java
public List<String> arrange() {
    return books.stream().sorted().collect(Collectors.toList());
}
```

Run the test cases again and all tests should be green.

Refactor

So far, we have modeled books as a simple String. But, we would like users to arrange books according to different attributes (author, published date, etc.). Thus, we should capture different attributes of a book. This warrants a new class.

Let's create a new Book class in the src/main/java/bookstoread package.

```java
package bookstoread;

import java.time.LocalDate;

public class Book {
    private final String title;
    private final String author;
    private final LocalDate publishedOn;

    public Book(String title, String author, LocalDate publishedOn) {
        this.title = title;
        this.author = author;
        this.publishedOn = publishedOn;
    }

    public String getTitle() {
        return title;
    }

    public String getAuthor() {
        return author;
    }

    public LocalDate getPublishedOn() {
        return publishedOn;
    }

    @Override
    public String toString() {
        return "Book{" +
                "title='" + title + '\'' +
                ", author='" + author + '\'' +
```

```
                ", publishedOn=" + publishedOn +
                '}';
    }
}
```

Let's change our tests to use Book class instead of String. We are using the same books in every test so we will extract them as part of test intialization.

```java
public class BookShelfSpec {

    private BookShelf shelf;
    private Book effectiveJava;
    private Book codeComplete;
    private Book mythicalManMonth;

    @BeforeEach
    void init() throws Exception {
        shelf = new BookShelf();
        effectiveJava = new Book("Effective Java", "Joshua Bloch",
        LocalDate.of(2008, Month.MAY, 8));
        codeComplete = new Book("Code Complete", "Steve McConnel",
        LocalDate.of(2004, Month.JUNE, 9));
        mythicalManMonth = new Book("The Mythical Man-Month", "Frederick
        Phillips Brooks", LocalDate.of(1975, Month.JANUARY, 1));
    }

    @Test
    public void shelfEmptyWhenNoBookAdded() {
        List<Book> books = shelf.books();
        assertTrue(books.isEmpty(), () -> "BookShelf should be empty.");
    }

    @Test
    public void bookshelfContainsTwoBooksWhenTwoBooksAdded() {
        shelf.add(effectiveJava, codeComplete);
        List<Book> books = shelf.books();
        assertEquals(2, books.size(), () -> "BookShelf should have two books.");
    }

    @Test
    public void emptyBookShelfWhenAddIsCalledWithoutBooks() {
        shelf.add();
        List<Book> books = shelf.books();
        assertTrue(books.isEmpty(), () -> "BookShelf should be empty.");
    }
```

```java
@Test
public void booksReturnedFromBookShelfIsImmutableForClient() {
    shelf.add(effectiveJava, codeComplete);
    List<Book> books = shelf.books();
    try {
        books.add(mythicalManMonth);
        fail(() -> "Should not be able to add book to books");
    } catch (Exception e) {
        assertTrue(e instanceof UnsupportedOperationException, () ->
        "Should throw UnsupportedOperationException.");
    }
}

@Test
void bookshelfArrangedByBookTitle() {
    shelf.add(effectiveJava, codeComplete, mythicalManMonth);
    List<Book> books = shelf.arrange();
    assertEquals(Arrays.asList(codeComplete, effectiveJava,
    mythicalManMonth), books, () -> "Books in a bookshelf should be
    arranged lexicographically by book title");
}

@Test
void booksInBookShelfAreInInsertionOrderAfterCallingArrange() {
    shelf.add(effectiveJava, codeComplete, mythicalManMonth);
    shelf.arrange();
    List<Book> books = shelf.books();
    assertEquals(Arrays.asList(effectiveJava, codeComplete, mythicalManMonth),
    books, () -> "Books in bookshelf are in insertion order");
}

}
```

This will make code compilation fail. So, we will have to fix the BookShelf to use Book instead of String. Replace the content of BookShelf with content shown in the code that follows:

```java
package bookstoread;

import java.util.*;
import java.util.stream.Collectors;

public class BookShelf {

    private final List<Book> books = new ArrayList<>();

    public List<Book> books() {
        return Collections.unmodifiableList(books);
    }
```

```java
    public void add(Book... booksToAdd) {
        Arrays.stream(booksToAdd).forEach(books::add);
    }

    public List<Book> arrange() {
        return books.stream().sorted().collect(Collectors.toList());
    }
}
```

This will fix all the compilation issues. Run the test cases again and you will find a couple of test cases related to the failed arrange use case. The exception message that you will see is shown in the code snippet that follows:

```
java.lang.ClassCastException: bookstoread.Book cannot be cast to java.lang.
Comparable
```

As you might have guessed, the reason is that Book class does not implement the Comparable interface. The sorted method used earlier assumes that the object you are sorting implements the Comparable interface. Change the Book to implement the Comparable interface as shown in the following code:

```java
public class Book implements Comparable<Book>{
    ... // removed for brevity

    @Override
    public int compareTo(Book that) {
        return this.title.compareTo(that.title);
    }
}
```

Run the test cases again and all the test cases will pass.

Now that everything is green, let's add a test case that allows the user to pass an arrangement criterion.

```java
@Test
void bookshelfArrangedByUserProvidedCriteria() {
    shelf.add(effectiveJava, codeComplete, mythicalManMonth);
    List<Book> books = shelf.arrange(Comparator.<Book>naturalOrder().reversed());
    assertEquals(
            asList(mythicalManMonth, effectiveJava, codeComplete),
            books,
            () -> "Books in a bookshelf are arranged in descending order of
            book title");
}
```

In the foregoing code, we are passing criteria from the test case. We want to arrange the bookshelf in reverse lexicographical order. This code will not compile. To make it compile, we will have to either change the existing arrange method to support passing in Comparator or add a new method, which supports criteria. We will add a new method and keep the old method for natural sorting (i.e., by title).

```
public List<Book> arrange() {
    return books.stream().sorted().collect(Collectors.toList());
}

public List<Book> arrange(Comparator<Book> criteria) {
    return null;
}
```

This will make the code compile, but our new test case will fail. To pass the test, we will change the code to the following:

```
public List<Book> arrange() {
    return books.stream().sorted().collect(Collectors.toList());
}

public List<Book> arrange(Comparator<Book> criteria) {
    return books.stream().sorted(criteria).collect(Collectors.toList());
}
```

Run the test cases again. This time all the test cases will be green. Take a moment and think about whether you can improve the foregoing code. You will notice that there is code duplication in the arrange methods. We can refactor the code as shown.

```
public List<Book> arrange() {
    return arrange(Comparator.naturalOrder());
}

public List<Book> arrange(Comparator<Book> criteria) {
    return books.stream().sorted(criteria).collect(Collectors.toList());
}
```

Run the test cases again and all the test cases will be again green. You can write one more test case to arrange the bookshelf by publication date.

Before we develop the next feature, let's talk about few more features of JUnit 5.

Disabled Tests

There are times when tests are broken for valid reasons. One of the ways to avoid the headache of ignoring the execution of failing tests is to use the @Disabled annotation. This is similar in intent to the JUnit 4 @Ignore annotation.

If a test is marked @Disabled, then JUnit engine will not run it. The annotation can also be used at class level. If a class is marked with the @Disabled annotation then it will skip all the tests inside the respective class. The @Disabled annotation takes a string as an optional parameter which will be printed on the console when the test is skipped. Also note that the JUnit engine prints overall statistics which contain numbers of ignored, failed, and total executed tests.

There are multiple ways we can ignore execution of test cases. We could remove the @Test annotation from the method/class. But, this will stop not only the execution of the test but also the discovery of the test. The test case will no longer be reported in JUnit statistics. It is far better to disable the test explicitly by using the @Disabled annotation rather than to delete it or remove the @Test annotation.

Let's mark the bookshelfArrangedByBookTitle test as @Disabled as shown in the code snippet that follows:

```java
@Disabled("Needs to implement Comparator")
@Test
void bookshelfArrangedByBookTitle() {
    shelf.add(effectiveJava, codeComplete, mythicalManMonth);
    List<Book> books = shelf.arrange();
    assertEquals(asList(codeComplete, effectiveJava, mythicalManMonth),
    books, () -> "Books in a bookshelf should be arranged lexicographically
    by book title");
}
```

Figure 3-4 illustrates how IntelliJ shows a disabled test.

Figure 3-4. *Disabled test*

AssertJ

Assertions are a vital part of test classes as they provide the result verification. Junit 5.0 provides a minimal set of assertion APIs. The JUnit platform is only concerned with assertion results and not with the assertion API. There are many third-party APIs that can help us to write expressive assertions. The previous version of JUnit used to embed Hamcrest library to provide this out of the box. But, the newer version has dropped Hamcrest; instead, it recommends using AssertJ to do the job.

AssertJ http://joel-costigliola.github.io/assertj/ is one of the de facto standards for writing assertions. It provides a rich fluent API to assert various aspects. Overall it offers the benefit of test case readability and maintenance.

In the bookshelfArrangedByUserProvidedCriteria test case, we tried to compare the order of books to an expected order. In our opinion, the test case has a small issue while validating the result. It is comparing two different collections to check elements order, but it is not validating if the elements in the results are ordered according to the provided comparator.

Let's say we change the comparator to the natural order. This will change the complete order of the result. But the failing test case will provide an error to correct the ordering to descending order.

```
Expected :[Book{title='The Mythical Man-Month', author='Frederick
Phillips Brooks', publishedOn=1975-01-01}, Book{title='Effective Java',
author='Joshua Bloch', publishedOn=2008-05-08}, Book{title='Code Complete',
author='Steve McConnel', publishedOn=2004-06-09}]

Actual   :[Book{title='Code Complete', author='Steve McConnel',
publishedOn=2004-06-09}, Book{title='Effective Java', author='Joshua
Bloch', publishedOn=2008-05-08}, Book{title='The Mythical Man-Month',
author='Frederick Phillips Brooks', publishedOn=1975-01-01}]
```

If we look at the test, the code is working as expected, but there is a bug in the asserting result. We can improve this a lot if we can validate that the result is ordered by the provided comparator rather than comparing the result with another collection. AssertJ allows us to do exactly that. Let's start by adding AssertJ dependency under the dependencies section of build.gradle.

```
dependencies {
    def junitVersion = '5.0.1'
    testCompile 'org.junit.jupiter:junit-jupiter-api:' + junitVersion
    testCompile 'org.junit.jupiter:junit-jupiter-engine:' + junitVersion
    testCompile 'org.assertj:assertj-core:3.8.0'
}
```

Now, let's modify the test case using the assertThat method of AssertJ library. We would like to make sure that the list is sorted using the provided Comparator. The assertThat assertion is part of org.assertj.core.api.Assertions class, so we must import the class before we can use the assertion.

```
import static org.assertj.core.api.Assertions.assertThat;
@Test
void bookshelfArrangedByUserProvidedCriteria() {
    shelf.add(effectiveJava, codeComplete, mythicalManMonth);
    Comparator<Book> reversed = Comparator.<Book>naturalOrder().reversed();
    List<Book> books = shelf.arrange(reversed);
    assertThat(books).isSortedAccordingTo(reversed);
}
```

The foregoing test case more accurately expresses our intent. Going further we will explore more of the AssertJ library to perform our verifications.

Using @DisplayName

We have written a few test cases for a couple of features we have developed. It is time to discuss one of the important aspects about tests–test case name. Naming a test case is one of the most difficult tasks for developers. The test should be named in such a manner that it should be easier to figure out why a test failed without looking at the test code.

> *What makes a clean test? Three things. Readability, readability, and readability. Readability is perhaps even more important in unit tests than it is in production code.*
>
> *- Uncle Bob*

Let's see how it impacts test cases. In the event of the test failure, the test case report for bookshelfArrangedByBookTitle looks as shown Figure 3-5.

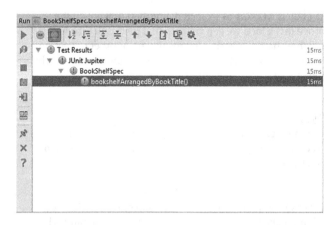

Figure 3-5. *Test failure message*

The failure is not descriptive. We need to look into logs or read test code to understand more about the failure. We could help ourselves by writing proper test names using @DisplayName annotation discussed in Chapter 2 (see Figure 3-6).

```
@Test
@DisplayName("bookshelf is arranged lexicographically by book title")
void bookshelfArrangedByBookTitle() {
    // Test case
    }
```

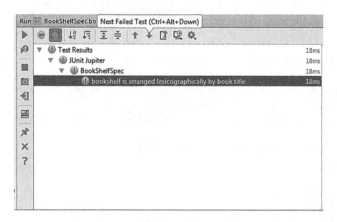

Figure 3-6. *Test DisplayName*

The test case name is quite descriptive, and tells us that the bookshelf is not arranged in its natural order. Let's try to give a meaningful description to all our tests. The resulting test run should look as shown in Figure 3-7.

▼ ⦿ Test Results	128ms
▼ ⦿ JUnit Jupiter	128ms
▼ ⦿ BookShelfSpec	128ms
⦿ bookshelf is empty when no book is added to it	16ms
⦿ bookshelf returns an immutable books collection to client	20ms
⦿ bookshelf is arranged lexicographically by book title	0ms
⦿ books inside bookshelf are grouped according to user provided criteria(	91ms
⦿ bookshelf contains two books when two books are added	0ms
⦿ empty bookshelf remains empty when add is called without books	0ms
⦿ bookshelf is arranged by user provided criteria (by book title lexicographi	0ms

Figure 3-7. *Passing test*

Third Feature

As a user, I should be able to group books in my bookshelf based on certain criteria

Write a Failing Test

In the section "Second Feature," we looked at how we can arrange a bookshelf based on user criteria. Now, the client wants us to support grouping within the bookshelf. They want us to initially support grouping by publication year and then later allow support for any user-provided criteria.

```
import static org.assertj.core.api.Assertions.assertThat;
@Test
@DisplayName("books inside bookshelf are grouped by publication year")
void groupBooksInsideBookShelfByPublicationYear() {
    shelf.add(effectiveJava, codeComplete, mythicalManMonth, cleanCode);

    Map<Year, List<Book>> booksByPublicationYear = shelf.
groupByPublicationYear();

    assertThat(booksByPublicationYear)
            .containsKey(Year.of(2008))
            .containsValues(Arrays.asList(effectiveJava, cleanCode));

    assertThat(booksByPublicationYear)
            .containsKey(Year.of(2004))
            .containsValues(singletonList(codeComplete));

    assertThat(booksByPublicationYear)
            .containsKey(Year.of(1975))
            .containsValues(singletonList(mythicalManMonth));
}
```

The foregoing code will not compile, as groupByPublication does not exist. Let's add the method as shown in the code snippet that follows:

```
public Map<Year, List<Book>> groupByPublicationYear() {
    return null;
}
```

This will make the code compilable, but we still need to write the implementation.

Make Test Pass

We will implement the test method by using the groupingBy collector as shown in the code snippet. The groupingBy collector takes the key function based on which we want to group our collection.

```
public Map<Year, List<Book>> groupByPublicationYear() {
    return books
            .stream()
            .collect(Collectors.groupingBy(book -> Year.of(book.
            getPublishedOn().getYear())));
}
```

This will make all tests green.

Refactor

Now, let's improve the code by making it generic so that clients can specify their own grouping criteria. This will make our API flexible and extensible. First, we will write the test case to group based on different criteria.

```
@Test
@DisplayName("books inside bookshelf are grouped according to user provided
criteria(group by author name)")
void groupBooksByUserProvidedCriteria() {
    shelf.add(effectiveJava, codeComplete, mythicalManMonth, cleanCode);
    Map<String, List<Book>> booksByAuthor = shelf.groupBy(Book::getAuthor);

    assertThat(booksByAuthor)
            .containsKey("Joshua Bloch")
            .containsValues(singletonList(effectiveJava));

    assertThat(booksByAuthor)
            .containsKey("Steve McConnel")
            .containsValues(singletonList(codeComplete));

    assertThat(booksByAuthor)
            .containsKey("Frederick Phillips Brooks")
            .containsValues(singletonList(mythicalManMonth));

    assertThat(booksByAuthor)
            .containsKey("Robert C. Martin")
            .containsValues(singletonList(cleanCode));
}
```

The code will not compile as the groupBy method does not exist.

```java
public <K> Map<K, List<Book>> groupBy(Function<Book, K> fx) {
    return books
            .stream()
            .collect(groupingBy(fx));
}
```

This will make all the test cases green. We will now refactor groupByPublicationYear so that it uses the groupBy method.

```java
public Map<Year, List<Book>> groupByPublicationYear() {
    return groupBy(book -> Year.of(book.getPublishedOn().getYear()));
}

public <K> Map<K, List<Book>> groupBy(Function<Book, K> fx) {
    return books
            .stream()
            .collect(groupingBy(fx));
}
```

Run the test cases and all tests should be green.

Nested Tests

In a well-written test suite, there will more than one test for different features of the application. In our example, so far, we implemented three features and at the same time we wrote close to 10 test cases. This often leads to a situation where our test class is exploding with test cases. JUnit 5 provides the @Nested annotation to provide a logical grouping of test cases in the form of static inner member classes. Each of the static inner classes can have its own life cycle methods. These methods will be executed in hierarchical order. Additionally, the nested classes can be marked with @DisplayName, giving us all the benefits of proper test names. There is no limit on the level of nesting you can do.

For our purposes, we can group individual features in the following manner:

```java
@DisplayName("A bookshelf")
public class BookShelfSpec {

    @BeforeEach
    void init() {
                    // Test case removed for brevity
    }

    @Nested
    @DisplayName("is empty")
    class IsEmpty {
```

```
    @Test
    @DisplayName("when no book is added to it")
    public void emptyBookShelfWhenNoBookAdded() {
                    // Test case removed for brevity
    }

    @Test
    @DisplayName("when add is called without books")
    void emptyBookShelfWhenAddIsCalledWithoutBooks() {
                    // Test case removed for brevity
    }

}

@Nested
@DisplayName("after adding books")
class BooksAreAdded {

    @Test
    @DisplayName("contains two books")
    void bookshelfContainsTwoBooksWhenTwoBooksAdded() {
                    // Test case removed for brevity
    }

    @Test
    @DisplayName("returns an immutable books collection to client")
    void bookshelfIsImmutableForClient() {
                            // Test case removed for brevity
        }
    }

}

    // Test case removed for brevity
}
```

Run all the test cases. The resulting tree should express the logical grouping as shown in Figure 3-8.

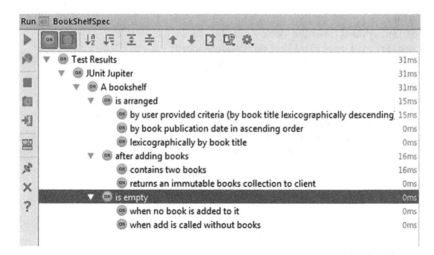

Figure 3-8. *Nested tests*

At the start of the chapter, we did not know the design of the Bookshelf. As we progressed through the features (and test cases) we found that it is a composition of books. Putting the test case first kept our solution simple and at the same time gave us freedom to use the right design choice for the problem at hand. As we develop more features using the test-first approach, we will see that they force us to build more components, thus propelling the evolution of the overall application design.

Summary

In this chapter, we took a deep dive into TDD using Junit 5.0. We experienced the Red-Green-Refactor cycle while building our application features. We used @BeforeEach to extract out our initialization procedures. We also used AssertJ to accurately express our intentions in test assertions. @DisplayName helped us to achieve better readability. As we evolved our test pack, we also organized it into logical groups using @Nested.

In the next chapter, we will add more features to the bookstoread application and will make use of JUnit features like dependency injection, interface default methods, and many more.

CHAPTER 4

Dependency Injection, Mocking, Testing Traits, and Grouping Tests

In the last chapter, we started building the bookstoread application. We added a few features to the application following TDD (test-driven development) practice and conforming to the Red-Green-Refactor cycle. In the process of writing the application, you learned about JUnit 5 core concepts and how you can start building your JUnit 5 test suite. This chapter will build upon the knowledge gained in the first three chapters and cover more advanced concepts of unit testing.

In any real application, multiple classes will collaborate to do the job. These dependencies need to be taken care of so that you can write clean and isolated tests. Most of the time test code is littered around with either test data setup or collaborator setup, both leading to tests that are difficult to read and comprehend.

In this chapter, we start by looking at dependency injection support introduced in JUnit 5, which can make our test data setup seamless and nonintrusive. Then, we will look at how mocking can help us to replace collaborators easily. We will use a mocking library, Mockito, which will do the work of creating and managing mock objects. It provides a higher-level API (application programming interface) that we use to write expectations that the mock should satisfy and we verify if those expectations are met. Mocking and dependency injection are linked to each other and you will see how dependency injection can help us inject mocks into our tests. We will end the chapter by looking at testing traits and support for defining test groups in JUnit 5.

Dependency Injection

One of the software design patterns that has been very useful in the last decade for simplifying software design is dependency injection (DI). According to Wikipedia,

> *Dependency injection is a technique whereby one object supplies the dependencies of another object.*

© Shekhar Gulati, Rahul Sharma 2017
S. Gulati, R. Sharma, *Java Unit Testing with JUnit 5*,
https://doi.org/10.1007/978-1-4842-3015-2_4

DI is a widely used pattern in the Java ecosystem. It was popularized by the Spring framework in early 2000. DI is all about making dependencies of an object explicit. They ease testing as you can inject stubs or mocks as dependencies, thus giving you control and power to test your component in isolation. DI prohibits the use of new (for creating objects) or static factory methods within a class. A component should expose methods/ fields which could be injected with the required objects. A DI provider will be responsible for creating instances of dependencies, injecting them into the required component, and managing their life cycle.

JUnit 5 provides support for DI with its extension mechanism. In JUnit 5, you can inject dependencies into either test methods or constructors. This is a big change from earlier versions of JUnit where test methods and constructors were required to be no-arg. This makes test code flexible as you can declare dependencies at places where you need them.

Let's look at how we can use DI to clean up BookShelfSpec tests we have written in Chapter 3. If you remember, our BookShelfSpec initialized test data in its @BeforeEach init method as shown in the code that follows:

```
public class BookShelfSpec {
    private BookShelf shelf;
    private Book effectiveJava;
    private Book codeComplete;
    private Book mythicalManMonth;
    private Book cleanCode;

    @BeforeEach
    void init() {
        shelf = new BookShelf();
        effectiveJava = new Book("Effective Java", "Joshua Bloch",
        LocalDate.of(2008, Month.MAY, 8));
        codeComplete = new Book("Code Complete", "Steve McConnel",
        LocalDate.of(2004, Month.JUNE, 9));
        mythicalManMonth = new Book("The Mythical Man-Month", "Frederick
        Phillips Brooks", LocalDate.of(1975, Month.JANUARY, 1));
        cleanCode = new Book("Clean Code", "Robert C. Martin", LocalDate.
        of(2008, Month.AUGUST, 1));
    }
    // rest removed for brevity
}
```

The aforementioned code has several problems.

- The test code is tightly coupled with test data. What if we want to run BookShelfSpec with different data based on some condition?

- We can't reuse test data. Most of the time multiple test classes need the same data. One way we can reuse test data is by creating a utility method that can be called to get the test data. This solution works fine, but it does not make programmer intent clear (i.e., to inject test data).

Now, that we understand the problem we are trying to solve let's learn how JUnit 5 can help us solve it. We will start by injecting test data into the init method as shown in the code that follows:

```
public class BookShelfSpec {

    private BookShelf shelf;
    private Book effectiveJava;
    private Book codeComplete;
    private Book mythicalManMonth;
    private Book cleanCode;

    @BeforeEach
    void init(Map<String, Book> books) {
        shelf = new BookShelf();
        this.effectiveJava = books.get("Effective Java");
        this.codeComplete = books.get("Code Complete");
        this.mythicalManMonth = books.get("The Mythical Man-Month");
        this.cleanCode = books.get("Clean Code");
    }
}
```

In the foregoing code, we injected Map<String, Book> to the init method. The key used for Map is book title and the value is Book itself. To minimize the changes in our tests, we assigned values to different Book instance variables. This will make sure all our tests continue to work as usual. Our tests are no longer concerned with creation of books test data; instead they expect the test data to be injected.

The DI API allows us to inject values into all phases of the JUnit life cycle. If there is a parameter in a test method annotated with @BeforeAll, @BeforeEach, @Test, @AfterEach, or @AfterAll, the framework would try to determine its value and inject it.

But how will JUnit 5 inject the test data into our init method?

JUnit 5 introduced the concept of ParameterResolver, which provides an API to resolve parameters at runtime. You can either use a built-in parameter resolver like TestInfoParameterResolver or provide your own resolver by implementing ParameterResolver interface. ParameterResolver is part of the JUnit 5 extension mechanism, which we will cover in a chapter 8. To make your test aware of your own custom resolver, you should annotate your test class with the ExtendWith annotation, providing it the resolver class as shown in the following code:

```
@DisplayName("A bookshelf")
@ExtendWith(BooksParameterResolver.class)
public class BookShelfSpec {
```

```
    private BookShelf shelf;
    private Book effectiveJava;
    private Book codeComplete;
    private Book mythicalManMonth;
    private Book cleanCode;

    @BeforeEach
    void init(Map<String, Book> books) {
        shelf = new BookShelf();
        this.effectiveJava = books.get("Effective Java");
        this.codeComplete = books.get("Code Complete");
        this.mythicalManMonth = books.get("The Mythical Man-Month");
        this.cleanCode = books.get("Clean Code");
    }
// rest removed for brevity
}
```

Let's look at what it takes to implement the BooksParameterResolver class.

```
import org.junit.jupiter.api.extension.ExtensionContext;
import org.junit.jupiter.api.extension.ParameterContext;
import org.junit.jupiter.api.extension.ParameterResolutionException;
import org.junit.jupiter.api.extension.ParameterResolver;

class BooksParameterResolver implements ParameterResolver {
    @Override
    public boolean supportsParameter(final ParameterContext
    parameterContext, final ExtensionContext extensionContext) throws
    ParameterResolutionException {
        return false;
    }
    @Override
    public Object resolveParameter(final ParameterContext
    parameterContext, final ExtensionContext extensionContext) throws
    ParameterResolutionException {
        return null;
    }
}
```

A class needs to implement the ParameterResolver interface so that it is considered for parameter resolution. The ParameterResolver interface has two methods that your custom implementation must implement.

- supportsParameter method validates if the implementation can provide the resolution for the asked parameter. The BooksParameterResolver needs to validate that it supports objects of type Map<String, Book>.

- resolveParameter method returns the value for the asked parameter. The BooksParameterResolver returns a Map containing books.

Let's look at the complete implementation of BooksParameterResolver in the following manner:

```java
import org.junit.jupiter.api.extension.ExtensionContext;
import org.junit.jupiter.api.extension.ParameterContext;
import org.junit.jupiter.api.extension.ParameterResolutionException;
import org.junit.jupiter.api.extension.ParameterResolver;

import java.lang.reflect.Parameter;
import java.time.LocalDate;
import java.time.Month;
import java.util.HashMap;
import java.util.Map;
import java.util.Objects;

class BooksParameterResolver implements ParameterResolver {
    @Override
    public boolean supportsParameter(final ParameterContext
    parameterContext, final ExtensionContext extensionContext) throws
    ParameterResolutionException {
        Parameter parameter = parameterContext.getParameter();
        return Objects.equals(parameter.getParameterizedType().
        getTypeName(), "java.util.Map<java.lang.String, bookstoread.Book>");
    }

    @Override
    public Object resolveParameter(final ParameterContext parameterContext,
final ExtensionContext extensionContext) throws ParameterResolutionException
{
        Map<String, Book> books = new HashMap<>();
        books.put("Effective Java", new Book("Effective Java", "Joshua
        Bloch", LocalDate.of(2008, Month.MAY, 8)));
        books.put("Code Complete", new Book("Code Complete", "Steve
        McConnel", LocalDate.of(2004, Month.JUNE, 9)));
        books.put("The Mythical Man-Month", new Book("The Mythical Man-
        Month", "Frederick Phillips Brooks", LocalDate.of(1975, Month.
        JANUARY, 1)));
        books.put("Clean Code", new Book("Clean Code", "Robert C. Martin",
        LocalDate.of(2008, Month.AUGUST, 1)));
        books.put("Refactoring: Improving the Design of Existing Code", new
        Book("Refactoring: Improving the Design of Existing Code", "Martin
        Fowler", LocalDate.of(2002, Month.MARCH, 9)));
        return books;
    }
}
```

In the foregoing code

- We implemented the supportsParameter method that checked whether the parameterized type of the parameter has the type of java.util.Map<java.lang.String, bookstoread.Book>. You must perform String check as that's the only way you can check for the parameterized type. ParameterContext makes use of the Java 8 Parameter API. Prior to JDK 8 there was no way to query information about method parameters.

- Next, we implemented the resolveParameter method, which returned a Map containing the test data.

Now, if you run BookShelfSpec all tests should be green as shown in Figure 4-1.

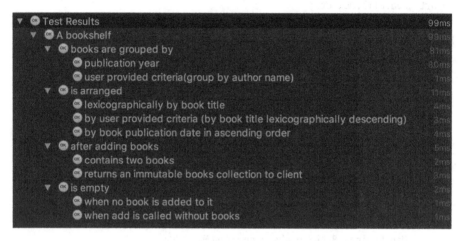

Figure 4-1. *Test execution after injecting test data*

Let's implement one more feature that we will use in next sections of this chapter.

Feature: Track Bookshelf Progress

As a user, I want to track the progress of my bookshelf based on the books I have read.

The feature is all about building a progress metric for a bookshelf. Users of bookstoread will keep on reading books and mark their progress. Consequently, we need to show them a progress indicator of how much they have accomplished. The complete metric consists of three items.

- **To-Do**: Indicating the percentage of books (of total books on shelf) a user has not read or started reading

- **Completed**: Indicating the percentage of books (of total books on shelf) a user has finished reading

- **In Progress**: Indicating the percentage of books (of total books on shelf) a user has read to some extent.

Let's say we have a bookshelf with the following four books:

- *Effective Java*
- *Code Complete*
- *Clean Code*
- *The Mythical Man-Month*

We have finished *Clean Code* and are in process of reading *Effective Java*. In such a case the complete metric should state 25% Completed, 25% In-Progress, and 50% To-Do.

Let's start building the feature by adding a test case for it. We would add a new Spec as shown in the following code:

```java
@DisplayName("A bookshelf progress")
public class BookShelfProgressSpec {
    private BookShelf shelf;
    private Book effectiveJava;
    private Book codeComplete;
    private Book mythicalManMonth;
    private Book cleanCode;
    private Book refactoring;

    @BeforeEach
    void init() {
        shelf = new BookShelf();
        effectiveJava = new Book("Effective Java", "Joshua Bloch",
        LocalDate.of(2008, Month.MAY, 8));
        // removed for brevity
    }

    @Test
    @DisplayName("is 0% completed and 100% to-read when no book is read yet")
    void progress100PercentUnread() {
        Progress progress = shelf.progress();
        assertThat(progress.completed()).isEqualTo(0);
        assertThat(progress.toRead()).isEqualTo(100);
    }
}
```

The foregoing test case will fail. We realize that the BookShelf returns an instance of progress class. Progress class holds the complete metric information. The progress encapsulates the required three metrics.

```java
public class Progress {
    private final int completed;
    private final int toRead;
    private final int inProgress;
    public Progress(int completed, int toRead, int inProgress) {
        this.completed = completed;
        this.toRead = toRead;
        this.inProgress = inProgress;
    }
    public int completed() {        return this.completed;     }
    public int toRead() {        return this.toRead;        }
    public int inProgress() {         return this.inProgress;        }
}
```

The BookShelf provides the progress API to determine the metric.

```java
public class BookShelf {
    //  ....
    // removed for brevity

  public Progress progress() {      return new Progress(0, 100, 0); }
}
```

Run the test again and it should be green now.

Now let's build another test case where we have read a few books.

```java
@Test
@DisplayName("is 40% completed and 60% to-read when 2 books are finished
and 3 books not read yet")
void progressWithCompletedAndToReadPercentages() {
    effectiveJava.startedReadingOn(LocalDate.of(2016, Month.JULY, 1));
    effectiveJava.finishedReadingOn(LocalDate.of(2016, Month.JULY, 31));
    cleanCode.startedReadingOn(LocalDate.of(2016, Month.AUGUST, 1));
    cleanCode.finishedReadingOn(LocalDate.of(2016, Month.AUGUST, 31));
    Progress progress = shelf.progress();
    assertThat(progress.completed()).isEqualTo(40);
    assertThat(progress.toRead()).isEqualTo(60);
}
```

Progress is just a reporting metric. But to build the number we need to track progress on each of the books, as done in the foregoing test case. Thus, we now have to add startedReadingOn and finishedReadingOn to the Book entity.

```java
public class Book implements Comparable<Book> {
// code removed for brevity
  public void startedReadingOn(LocalDate startedOn) {
  this.startedReadingOn = startedOn; }
```

```
public void finishedReadingOn(LocalDate finishedOn) {
this.finishedReadingOn = finishedOn; }
public boolean isRead() {     return startedReadingOn != null &&
finishedReadingOn != null; }
}
```

Take notice of the isRead method. We will use the method to process the list of books in a BookShelf. We can convert the List<Books> in a Stream and then apply a filter using the isRead method to get the number of read books.

```
int booksRead = Long.valueOf(books.stream().filter(Book::isRead).count()).
intValue();
```

Let's implement the progress method of BookShelf based on what we have so far.

```
public Progress progress() {
    int booksRead = Long.valueOf(books.stream().filter(Book::isRead).
    count()).intValue();
    int booksToRead = books.size() - booksRead;
    int percentageCompleted = booksRead * 100 / books.size();
    int percentageToRead = booksToRead * 100 / books.size();
    return new Progress(percentageCompleted, percentageToRead, 0);
}
```

This should make the test green again. Up to this point we have added progress indicators for Completed and To-Do. Now, let's add few test cases to compute books In Progress. In order to do this, add isProgress() to the Book class and use it to filter the stream of Books.

Also, along similar lines, we can add a test case that covers a scenario in which all books in a BookShelf are finished. Figure 4-2 shows successful execution of all the test cases related to bookshelf progress.

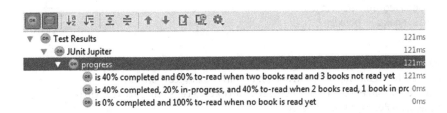

Figure 4-2. BookShelf progress sucessful test execution

So, are we done with the feature? Not completely, we have written tests and code to make them pass. We still need to refactor our tests to make improvements. If we look at our test case then we will find that there is really nothing left to improve upon. But now let us compare BookShelfProgressSpec with BookShelfSpec (written in Chapter 3). We find duplicate test data setup. A BookShelf needs books to work. We should use knowledge of DI that we gained in the section "Dependency Injection" to make this code better.

Let's annotate BookShelfProgressSpec with ExtendWith annotation and provide it BooksParameterResolver.

```
@DisplayName("progress")
@ExtendWith(BooksParameterResolver.class)
class BookShelfProgressSpec {
// rest removed for Brevity
}
```

Run BookShelfProgressSpec and all test cases should be green. This way we didn't have to duplicate test data for both our test cases. ParameterResolver made it easy for us to reuse data setup. Also, if required we can switch the data provided by the resolver at runtime in case we want to test with some other data. Our test case does not care how Map<String, Book> is provided to it. Data could be read from the database, read from a file, or created in memory.

Caching Test Data

The JUnit 5 extension mechanism creates a single instance of parameter resolver for a test class, but it calls the resolve method for each injection point invocation. In our case, we have a single injection point @BeforeEach init method, but as per the life cycle of @BeforeEach, it is called for each test case. This means that for each test execution, we have a new copy of test data. If your tests do not change the state of data and are read-only, then you can avoid creating new copy each time by storing the Map<String, Book> in an instance variable of BooksParameterResolver class as shown in the following code:

```
class BooksParameterResolver implements ParameterResolver {
    private final Map<String, Book> books;
    public BooksParameterResolver() {
        Map<String, Book> books = new HashMap<>();
        books.put("Effective Java", new Book("Effective Java", "Joshua
        Bloch", LocalDate.of(2008, Month.MAY, 8)));
    // removed for brevity
     this.books = books;
    }

    @Override
    public boolean supportsParameter(final ParameterContext
    parameterContext, final ExtensionContext extensionContext) throws
    ParameterResolutionException {
// removed for brevity
}
    @Override
    public Map<String, Book> resolveParameter(final ParameterContext
    parameterContext, final ExtensionContext extensionContext) throws
    ParameterResolutionException {
        return books;
    }
}
```

If you run the all the tests, you will notice that one of the tests fails, as shown in the screenshot in Figure 4-3.

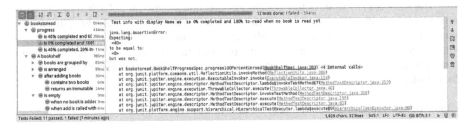

Figure 4-3. *Test failure when caching test data*

The reason for the test failure is that one of the test cases in the suite changed the state of the test data. This test expected a clean copy of test data so it failed.

The chain gang anti-pattern: This anti-pattern refers to the fact that a bunch of unit tests must be processed in a particular order or as a bunch. Each executed test does some work for the next one and thus they depend on each other.

Using ExtensionContext Store

So far, in our test cases, we injected test data in the @BeforeEach init method and then stored different books in the instance variable. What if we wanted to inject the same test data in both the init and test methods so that we don't have to store it in a test class instance variable. The two approaches that we have seen so far do not solve this use case.

- Creating test data for each invocation will pass a new copy of test data.

- Caching test data for all the tests in a test class will fail when another test changes the state of test data.

To look for a possible solution, let's delve into the details of the JUnit API. The resolve method takes two arguments.

- **ParameterContext**: It contains the details of the parameter being asked for.

- **ExtensionContext**: It contains the context of the current test. Each test execution creates its own ExentionContext. The context contains details like test method, id, and so on.

Besides the test-specific details, the context also offers ExtenContext.Store, which could be used to hold data for the particular context execution.

- Store getStore()

- Store getStore(Namespace namespace)

The Store is a key value holder which offers get and put methods. Each Store instance is uniquely identified by a namespace, which can be used to create a new store. In each test's ExtensionContext there is a default namespace available, but it is advisable to create a custom namespace to uniquely identify your data and avoid any data corruption issues. So now modify the BooksParameterResolver to use an ExtensionContext.Store for a custom Books namespace and serve the array of books from there.

```
class BooksParameterResolver implements ParameterResolver {

    @Override
    public Object resolveParameter(final ParameterContext
    parameterContext, final ExtensionContext extensionContext) throws
    ParameterResolutionException {
        ExtensionContext.Store store = extensionContext.
        getStore(ExtensionContext.Namespace.create(Book.class));
        return store.getOrComputeIfAbsent("books", k -> getBooks());
    }

// removed for brevity

}
```

Run all the tests and verify that they are green. Now, that the test code is in good shape, we can start working on the next feature.

Before we move to the next section on mocking, let's build another feature that will help us apply mocking in a real scenario.

Feature: Search BookShelf

As a user, I should be able to search my bookshelf. The search results can be filtered by different attributes of the book like author and published date.

The next feature adds the searching capability to the BookShelf. As a user, we would like to find a particular title in our BookShelf. The search should be based on the partial text. This can lead to many results for a term, so hints can be passed in the form of additional information like published date or the author's name to filter down the results to the required ones.

Let us start on this feature by adding a plain vanilla title-based search to the BookShelf.

```
@Nested
@DisplayName("search")
 class BookShelfSeachSpec {
     @BeforeEach
      void setup() {
```

```
        shelf.add(codeComplete, effectiveJava, mythicalManMonth, cleanCode);
    }

    @Test
    @DisplayName(" should find books with title containing text")
    void shouldFindBooksWithTitleContainingText() {
        List<Book> books = shelf.findBooksByTitle("code");
        assertThat(books.size()).isEqualTo(2);
    }
}
```

We will leave out the details of the findBooksByTitle method. The reader must try to add an implementation which makes the foregoing test case pass.

Now let's enhance the API by adding the required hints. In the feature description, a user may wish to search on published date, so we should add a test case for the same.

```
@Test
    @DisplayName(" should find books with title containing text and published
    after specified date.")
    void shouldFilterSearchedBooksBasedOnPublishedDate() {
        List<Book> books = shelf.findBooksByTitle("code", b ->
        b.getPublishedOn().isBefore(LocalDate.of(2014, 12, 31)));
        assertThat(books.size()).isEqualTo(2);
    }
```

Here we are using a new variant of the findBooksByTitle method. Now go back to the BookShelf and add the overloaded method.

```
    public List<Book> findBooksByTitle(String title) {
      return findBooksByTitle(title, b -> true);
}

public List<Book> findBooksByTitle(String title, Predicate<Book> filter) {
        return books.stream()
          .filter(b -> b.getTitle().toLowerCase().contains(title))
          .filter(filter)
          .collect(toList());
    }
```

Let's run our tests. They are green, so, shall we proceed further? Perhaps add a test for author name? Let's first ask if the two-argument findBooksByTitle API is correct? The foregoing implementation is low level and cannot adequately represent the concept of filters. The design does not tell anything about filters and their use. Thus, even though the API works and serves the purpose, it does not meet the required criteria.

■ **Primitive Obsession**   This is a design smell which is about representing business domain concepts as low-level types. It refers to the fact that the system is missing required abstractions. In such scenarios, we build interactions based on primitives, thus exposing too many details and making it hard to understand and maintain.

In the aforementioned scenario, we need to build the concept of a BookFilter. There could be variants of the BookFilter which can perform a different kind of filtering.

```
public interface BookFilter {
    boolean apply(Book b);
}
```

Also modify the findBooksByTitle API to use the BookFilter instead of the java. util.function.Predicate.

```
public List<Book> findBooksByTitle(String title, BookFilter filter) {
        return books.stream()
            .filter(b -> b.getTitle().toLowerCase().contains(title))
        .filter(b -> filter.apply(b))
            .collect(toList());
}
```

Our test cases work fine without any single line of change. We have added a functional interface BookFilter, and the lambda expression in the test case provides the required implementation of the interface (see Figure 4-4).

Figure 4-4. *Successful test execution of search-related tests*

Now that we have added the concept of BookFilter we would like to build few filters like a published year filter, where we will filter books published after the specified year. Let's add a simple test case as BookPublishedFilterSpec.

```
class BookFilterSpec {
    private Book cleanCode;
    private Book codeComplete;

    @BeforeEach
    void init() {
```

```
    cleanCode = new Book("Clean Code", "Robert C. Martin", LocalDate.
    of(2008, Month.AUGUST, 1));
    codeComplete = new Book("Code Complete", "Steve McConnel", LocalDate.
    of(2004, Month.JUNE, 9));
  }

  @Nested
  @DisplayName("book published date")
  class BookPulishedFilterSpec{
    @Test
    @DisplayName("is after specified year")
    void validateBookPublishedDatePostAskedYear(){
      BookFilter filter = BookPublishedYearFilter.After(2007);
      assertTrue(filter.apply(cleanCode));
      assertFalse(filter.apply(codeComplete));
    }
  }
}
```

In the previous test case, we are testing the BookPublishedYearFilter. The filter makes sure that a book must be published after the specified year. So now add an implementation for the same and make the test case green.

```
class BookPublishedYearFilter implements BookFilter {
  private LocalDate startDate;

  static BookPublishedYearFilter After(int year) {
    BookPublishedYearFilter filter = new BookPublishedYearFilter();
    filter.startDate = LocalDate.of(year, 12, 31);
    return filter;
  }

  @Override
  public boolean apply(final Book b) {
    return b.getPublishedOn().isAfter(startDate);
  }
}
```

Similar to the lines of After year filter, we would like to add a Before year filter, to find out books published before the specified year. As an exercise, this is left to the reader.

Run the test cases and make sure that all tests are green (see Figure 4-5).

Figure 4-5. *Succesful test execution*

Now that we have multiple filters, we would like to build a `CompositeFilter` which could be used to combine multiple filters into one single filter. Let's start by adding a test case for the same.

```
@Test
  @DisplayName("Composite criteria is based on multiple filters")
  void shouldFilterOnMultiplesCriteria(){
    CompositeFilter compositeFilter = new CompositeFilter();
    compositeFilter.addFilter( b -> false);
    assertFalse(compositeFilter.apply(cleanCode));
  }
```

Add the composite filter implementation to meet the test criteria.

```
class CompositeFilter implements BookFilter {
    private List<BookFilter> filters;

    CompositeFilter() {
      filters = new ArrayList<>();
    }

    @Override
     public boolean apply(final Book b) {
      return filters.stream()
        .map(bookFilter -> bookFilter.apply(b))
        .reduce(true, (b1, b2) -> b1 && b2);
    }

    void addFilter(final BookFilter bookFilter) {
      filters.add(bookFilter);
    }
  }
```

The test case works, but there is a nagging question. Did the composite filter invoke the passed filters? Also, how can we add a test case for scenarios which involve invocations of only a few of the filters? Shall we try to build some tests for the same?

```
@DisplayName("Composite criteria does not invoke after first failure")
   void shouldNotInvokeAfterFirstFailure(){
      CompositeFilter compositeFilter = new CompositeFilter();
      compositeFilter.addFilter( b -> false);
      compositeFilter.addFilter( b -> true);
      assertFalse(compositeFilter.apply(cleanCode));
   }

@DisplayName("Composite criteria invokes all filters")
   void shouldInvokeAllFilters(){
      CompositeFilter compositeFilter = new CompositeFilter();
      compositeFilter.addFilter( b -> true);
      compositeFilter.addFilter( b -> true);
      assertTrue(compositeFilter.apply(cleanCode));
   }
```

In all the foregoing scenarios, it is hard to determine the point at which the filter invocation has happened.

Mocking

Until now in all our test cases where we passed the BookFilter, we used a lambda expression. The expression created an implementation of the BookFilter and passed it to the respective methods. These test-generated implementations are known as mock objects (i.e., a substitute for an actual system implementation). One of the objectives while creating mocks is to test the required behaviors. But the lambda expression-based mock allowed us only to validate the test result, not the mock interaction; that is, we could not validate if the mocked instance was invoked or not. The problem is more apparent in the CompositeFilter where we have a chain of filters.

Using mocks is a good idea, as it allows us to test the system in isolation. But the quality of our mocks is not good enough. We need to improve our mocks to keep track of interactions. We can keep track of this information in an external data structure like a Map.

```
@Test
@DisplayName("Composite criteria invokes multiple filters")
void shouldFilterOnMultiplesCriteria(){
   CompositeFilter compositeFilter = new CompositeFilter();
   final Map<Integer, Boolean> invocationMap = new HashMap<>();
   compositeFilter.addFilter( b -> {
     invocationMap.put(1,true);
     return true;
   });
   compositeFilter.apply(cleanCode);
}
```

The aforementioned solution looks ugly. It has so many low-level details and makes the test case hard to understand. As an alternative, we can build a MockFilter abstraction where we can keep track of the invocation.

```
class MockedFilter implements BookFilter {
  boolean returnValue;
  boolean invoked;
  MockedFilter(boolean returnValue){
    this.returnValue=returnValue;
  }
  @Override
  public boolean apply(Book b) {
    invoked= true;
    return returnValue;
  }
}
```

The problem with this approach is that we are trying to reinvent the wheel. In any project, the requirement of mocking would increase as we develop more components. Thus, using mocks for everything soon becomes quite unmanageable.

Thus, as a final solution to the foregoing problem, we should try to work with any one of the available Mocking frameworks. Here we will be working with Mockito. Let's first add its dependency in our build.gradle

```
dependencies {
    def junitVersion = '5.0.1'
    testCompile 'org.junit.jupiter:junit-jupiter-api:' + junitVersion
    testCompile 'org.junit.jupiter:junit-jupiter-engine:' + junitVersion
    testCompile 'org.assertj:assertj-core:3.5.2'
    testCompile 'org.mockito:mockito-core:2.+'
}
```

This will add Mockito libraries to our project's test classpath. In order to work with it, we must take the following steps:

- Generate mocks by using the Mockito.*mock*() API.

- Record the required invocations using Mockito.when. The when API can be linked with a thenXXX API to return a value. These recorded interactions will be replayed when the test case makes the required calls.

- At the end of the test verify all interactions that happened with the mock.

So now our test case for the composite filter looks as follows:

```
@Test
@DisplayName("Composite criteria does not invoke after first failure")
void shouldNotInvokeAfterFirstFailure() {
    CompositeFilter compositeFilter = new CompositeFilter();

    BookFilter invokedMockedFilter = Mockito.mock(BookFilter.class);
    Mockito.when(invokedMockedFilter.apply(cleanCode)).thenReturn(false);
    compositeFilter.addFilter(invokedMockedFilter);

    BookFilter nonInvokedMockedFilter = Mockito.mock(BookFilter.class);
    Mockito.when(nonInvokedMockedFilter.apply(cleanCode)).thenReturn(true);
    compositeFilter.addFilter(nonInvokedMockedFilter);

    assertFalse(compositeFilter.apply(cleanCode));
    Mockito.verify(invokedMockedFilter).apply(cleanCode);
    Mockito.verifyZeroInteractions(nonInvokedMockedFilter);
}

@Test
@DisplayName("Composite criteria invokes all filters")
void shouldInvokeAllFilters() {
    CompositeFilter compositeFilter = new CompositeFilter();
    BookFilter firstInvokedMockedFilter = Mockito.mock(BookFilter.class);
    Mockito.when(firstInvokedMockedFilter.apply(cleanCode)).
    thenReturn(true);
    compositeFilter.addFilter(firstInvokedMockedFilter);

    BookFilter secondInvokedMockedFilter = Mockito.mock(BookFilter.class);
    Mockito.when(secondInvokedMockedFilter.apply(cleanCode)).
    thenReturn(true);
    compositeFilter.addFilter(secondInvokedMockedFilter);
    assertTrue(compositeFilter.apply(cleanCode));
    Mockito.verify(firstInvokedMockedFilter).apply(cleanCode);
    Mockito.verify(secondInvokedMockedFilter).apply(cleanCode);
}
```

Let's run it! But now there is a failing test as shown in Figure 4-6.

Figure 4-6. Mocking detected failure

Well, if we look at the failure message, it clearly states that no interactions were expected, but the mock was invoked by a lambda expression. We did not expect this but the behavior of the CompositeFilter is otherwise. It always invokes the complete chain of the filters irrespective of the end result. For our business scenario, the behavior does not make much difference. But the test case serves as a good documentation of what is expected from the filter. Let's modify the test case to make it green.

In the foregoing section, we used Mockito to discover the behavior of our CompositeFilter. The section was aimed at a brief introduction to the mocking framework and does not cover it in detail. Refer to Mockito documentation to learn more about its offerings.

Testing Traits

Now that, we have a bunch of BookFilters, we can expect a set of common behaviors from them. Each of the filters is having its own test scenario. But for all of them, we are missing boundary condition test cases. Should a filter fail or throw back an exception if invoked with a null book?

In such cases, where common behavior is expected, we should avoid building separate tests for each of the filters. Instead of adding separate test methods for each of the filters, we can have a single test case for the foregoing scenario and add it as a default method of an interface. The method must be annotated with @Test.

```
interface FilterBoundaryTests {
    BookFilter get();

    @Test
    @DisplayName("should not fail for null book.")
    default void nullTest() {
        assertThat(get().apply(null)).isFalse();
    }
}
```

It is important to note that the default method of the interface implements the complete test case. Things like subject under test can be asked as an interface method which will be implemented by the implementing class. We can now implement the previous interface in our existing FilterSpecs, thereby implementing the get() method in each test class. As a result, the nullTest() will become part of each test class.

```
class BookPublishedBeforeFilterSpec implements FilterBoundaryTests {
    BookFilter filter;

    @BeforeEach
    void init() {
        filter = BookPublishedYearFilter.Before(2007);
    }

    @Override
    public BookFilter get() {
        return filter;
    }
    // rest removed for Brevity
}
```

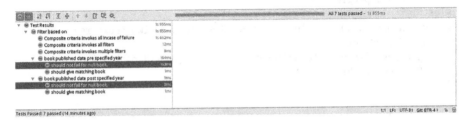

Figure 4-7. *Default Tests*

In addition to test methods, an interface can have default methods for @BeforeEach and @AfterEach life cycle events. Such life cycle methods will be invoked for every test in the test class.

Default methods cannot take part in @BeforeAll and @AfterAll life cycle events. Only static methods of an interface can take part in these events.

Grouping Tests by Tags

In most of the projects, tests have various characteristics. Some tests are slow, some are fast, and some are environment specific, for example. Thus, we would like to distinguish between these tests in our suite and organize them in similar groups. The idea behind this grouping is that we can select a group and execute it as per our requirement. JUnit 5 enables us to mark these characteristics on our tests by using the @Tag annotation. A test can be tagged "slow," "fast," "nightly," and so on. After marking a test class/method with a tag, we can select the tag in our integrated development environment (IDE)/build tool runner. This would select all the tests marked with the required tag and execute them. The tags annotation is a java.lang.annoatation.Repeatable annotation. Thus, we can add the annotation multiple times to a test method/class, thereby adding multiple metadata to it.

87

While we were writing this book, IntelliJ Idea had not provided any option to work with tags. It is a still undergoing milestone releases to support all features of JUnit 5.

It is important to note that the tag info is restricted to the Junit test runner. The meta-information is also part of the TestInfo object. The object could be injected into life cycle methods to take some relevant actions.

```
@BeforeEach
 void setup(Book[] books, TestInfo info) {
     System.out.println(" Test tags are :  "+ info.getTags());
 }

 @Tag("nightly")
 @Tag("generate-progress")
 @Test
 @DisplayName("is 40% completed and 60% to-read when two books read and 3
 books not read yet")
 void progressWithCompletedAndToReadPercentages(Book[] books) {
   // Removed for Brevity
 }
```

Junit 4 API contained the @Category annotation to mark tests with meta-information which could be used to build test groups. The API is no longer available in JUnit 5.

Summary

In this chapter, we enhanced the bookstoread application by adding a couple of new features. In the process, we worked with dependency injection and used assumptions to validate our test preconditions. We took a crash course on the JUnit Extension model. This book will cover the topic in more detail in future chapters.

We found out that business domain concepts should be expressed as abstractions in the system. All such abstractions can be unit tested by Mocking. We discovered that we can build mock implementations for our interfaces, but it is more efficient to use a mocking framework like Mockito. In the end, we discussed how default methods in interfaces can be used to test common behaviors of our abstractions.

In Chapter 5, we will learn about exception handling improvements added in JUnit 5.

CHAPTER 5

Testing Exceptions

So far in this book, we have not talked much about handling exceptions with JUnit 5. As programmers, we know exceptions will happen and we must verify that exceptions get thrown when expected. In this chapter, you'll learn how to use various ways supported by JUnit 5 to work with exceptions. We will end the chapter by talking about JUnit 5 support of repeated test execution. Repeated test execution is helpful when you have to work with flaky tests. A test is flaky when it exhibits both a passing and a failing result with the same code base.

Context Setting

Let's consider a use case to ensure that BookShelf throws an exception when more books are added than its capacity. As you can see in the code that follows, the BookShelfCapacityReached exception is thrown when we try to add more books than BookShelf capacity.

```java
public void add(Book... booksToAdd) throws BookShelfCapacityReached {
    Arrays.stream(booksToAdd).forEach(book -> {
        if (books.size() == capacity) {
            throw new BookShelfCapacityReached(String.format("BookShelf
            capacity of %d is reached. You can't add more books.", this.
            capacity));
        }
        books.add(book);
    });
}
```

Primitive Way: Using the try-catch-fail

When working with a code that might throw an exception, first you have to create a condition that will throw an exception and then you have to verify that it is the expected exception. Additionally, you might want to verify the message contained in the exception. In the code shown previously, we can create the exception condition in a test by adding a book to the BookShelf after reaching its capacity of two.

© Shekhar Gulati, Rahul Sharma 2017
S. Gulati, R. Sharma, *Java Unit Testing with JUnit 5*,
https://doi.org/10.1007/978-1-4842-3015-2_5

```
@Test
void throwsExceptionWhenBooksAreAddedAfterCapacityIsReached() {
    BookShelf bookShelf = new BookShelf(2);
    bookShelf.add(effectiveJava, codeComplete);
    bookShelf.add(mythicalManMonth);
}
```

Running the code will fail the test as an exception will be thrown by the bookShelf. add(mythicalManMonth) line. This is not what we want. The test case not only has to raise an exception but also verify the exception as well. The expected behavior of the code is to raise an exception; thus the test should succeed and not fail.

The classic approach to work with exceptions is to use Java's inbuilt try-catch mechanism. The try block will wrap the code that throws an exception and the catch block allows us to catch the exception thrown by the code.

Always capture a specific exception in the try-catch block.

```
@Test
void throwsExceptionWhenBooksAreAddedAfterCapacityIsReached() {
    BookShelf bookShelf = new BookShelf(2);
    bookShelf.add(effectiveJava, codeComplete);
    try {
        bookShelf.add(mythicalManMonth);
    } catch (BookShelfCapacityReached expected) {
        assertEquals("BookShelf capacity of 2 is reached. You can't add more
        books.", expected.getMessage());
    }
}
```

In the aforementioned code, we wrapped the bookShelf.add statement in a try-catch block. We caught the BookShelfCapacityReached exception and verified that message is the expected one.

Is the foregoing test case complete? No, it will work even when no exception is thrown by the bookshelf.add statement. To make sure that the test fails in case an exception is not raised, we call the org.junit.jupiter.api.Assertions.fail method to achieve the expected behavior as shown in the code that follows:

```
@Test
void throwsExceptionWhenBooksAreAddedAfterCapacityIsReached() {
    BookShelf bookShelf = new BookShelf(2);
    bookShelf.add(effectiveJava, codeComplete);
    try {
        bookShelf.add(mythicalManMonth);
        fail("Should throw BookShelfCapacityReached exception as more books
        are added than shelf capacity.");
```

```
    } catch (BookShelfCapacityReached expected) {
        assertEquals("BookShelf capacity of 2 is reached. You can't add more
        books.", expected.getMessage());
    }
}
```

The try-catch-fail approach to testing exceptions has existed since JUnit's beginning. It is still a valid approach, but most of the time you will be better off using the modern approaches.

JUnit 4 Way: @Test Annotation and Rule API

You will agree that the try-catch-fail approach discussed previously is verbose and ugly. It leads to code that is hard to read and maintain. Prior to JUnit 5, the two recommended ways to work with exceptions were

- **Using @Test annotation expected attribute**: The previous version of the JUnit @Test annotation supported specifying an argument that identifies the type of expected exception. This made the testing exception simple, as shown in the following code.

```
@Test(expected=BookShelfCapacityReached.class)
public void
throwsExceptionWhenBooksAreAddedAfterCapacityIsReached() {
    BookShelf bookShelf = new BookShelf(2);
    bookShelf.add(effectiveJava, codeComplete);
    bookShelf.add(mythicalManMonth);
}
```

  If the BookShelfCapacityReached exception is thrown during test execution, the foregoing test passes. Otherwise, the test will fail.

  There are two drawbacks to this approach

  - You can't narrow down the piece of code that throws the exception

  - You can't assert the exception message

  The JUnit 5 @Test annotation does not have the expected attribute, so this approach will not work.

- **Using ExpectedException Rule:** Another more extensible approach supported by JUnit 4 is to use the ExpectedException rule. JUnit Rule API provides more control over what happened during the code execution. ExpectedException is one of the inbuilt rules provided by JUnit 4 itself.

```
public class BookShelfSpecWithRules {

    @Rule
    public ExpectedException expectedException =
ExpectedException.none();

    @Test
    void throwsExceptionWhenBooksAreAddedAfterCapacityIsReached() {
        BookShelf bookShelf = new BookShelf(1);
        expectedException.expect(BookShelfCapacityReached.class);
        expectedException.expectMessage("BookShelf capacity of 1
        is reached. You can't add more books.");

        bookShelf.add(effectiveJava, codeComplete);
    }
}
```

In the foregoing code, we first created an instance of
ExpectedException and then we told the expectedException
rule what we expect during the execution of the test.

The JUnit 4 rule mechanism allows us to verify both thrown
exception and message. This approach also suffers from the
limitation that we can't narrow down the piece of code that
threw an exception. This means your test might be passing for
the wrong reason.

JUnit 5 has limited support for the Rule API. The ExpectedException rule is
supported by JUnit 5. This means you can still run your existing tests written using the
ExpectedException Rule API. We will cover it later in this chapter.

JUnit 5 Way: Using assertThrows Assertion Method

The JUnit 5 Assertions class provides an org.junit.jupiter.api.Assertions.
assertThrows method that lets you write code to verify both the exception and the
associated message in a clean and readable manner. It also allows you to narrow down
the code that throws the exception, avoiding the issues with JUnit 4 approaches. The code
that follows refactors the test case to use the assertThrows method:

```
@Test
void throwsExceptionWhenBooksAreAddedAfterCapacityIsReached() {
    BookShelf bookShelf = new BookShelf(2);
    bookShelf.add(effectiveJava, codeComplete);
    BookShelfCapacityReached throwException = assertThrows(BookShelfCapacity
    Reached.class, () -> bookShelf.add(mythicalManMonth));
    assertEquals("BookShelf capacity of 2 is reached. You can't add more
    books.", throwException.getMessage());
}
```

The assertThrows method takes these arguments–expected Exception class and a lambda expression of the type org.junit.jupiter.api.function.Executable.

Executable is used to encapsulate a piece of code which can throw an exception. The Executable functional interface is similar to the Java inbuilt java.lang.Runnable interface, the only difference being that Runnable does not use a throws clause in its declaration. This means your lambda expression must catch the checked exception and then rethrow the unchecked exception. You can avoid this hassle by writing your own functional interface that uses a throws clause. This is what an Executable interface does. The other advantage of creating a functional interface is to allow the use of a name corresponding to your domain. Executable tells us that this lambda encapsulates a code execution.

```
@FunctionalInterface
public interface Executable {
        void execute() throws Throwable;
}
```

assertThrows returns the caught exception that we used in the next statement to assert the exception message as shown in the preceding code example.

Using JUnit 4 ExpectedException Rule with JUnit 5

JUnit 5 has limited support for JUnit 4 Rule API support. This means you can still write/run tests using the JUnit 4 Rule API support. The support for Rule API is defined in the junit-jupiter-migration-support module. For any new test, you should use the assertThrows method, but if you have a JUnit 4 code base then you can rely on this extension. To use Rule API, first add the dependency to your build tool. If you are using Gradle, then please add the following to your build.gradle file.

```
testCompile 'org.junit.jupiter:junit-jupiter-migrationsupport:5.0.1'
```

Maven users can add following to their pom.xml.

```
<dependency>
    <groupId>org.junit.jupiter</groupId>
    <artifactId>junit-jupiter-migrationsupport</artifactId>
    <version>5.0.1</version>
  <scope>test</scope>
</dependency>
```

After adding the dependency, you have to enable Rule API support in your test case by annotating your test class with EnableRuleMigrationSupport annotation as shown in the code that follows.

```
import org.junit.Rule;
import org.junit.jupiter.api.Test;
import org.junit.jupiter.migrationsupport.rules.EnableRuleMigrationSupport;
import org.junit.platform.runner.JUnitPlatform;
```

93

```
import org.junit.rules.ExpectedException;
import org.junit.runner.RunWith;

@EnableRuleMigrationSupport
public class BookShelfSpecWithRules {
    @Rule
    public ExpectedException expectedException = ExpectedException.none();

    @Test
    void throwsExceptionWhenBooksAreAddedAfterCapacityIsReached() {
        BookShelf bookShelf = new BookShelf(1);
        expectedException.expect(BookShelfCapacityReached.class);
        expectedException.expectMessage("BookShelf capacity of 1 is reached.
        You can't add more books.");
        bookShelf.add(effectiveJava, codeComplete);
    }
}
```

Apart from adding EnableRuleMigrationSupport annotation, you don't have to make any changes in your code base.

Now, you can run the test case and it will succeed.

Exception Handling Extension

As mentioned in Chapter 4, JUnit 5 provides extensibility using its Extension API. We will cover the extension API in detail in Chapter 7 JUnit 5 provides plug points for developers by using the extension API. The TestExecutionExceptionHandler Extension interface is called when the test results in an exception. Let's consider a use case where we need to log all the exceptions that are thrown by the test cases. We can write LoggingTestExecutionExceptionHandler as shown in the code that follows:

```
import org.junit.jupiter.api.extension.TestExecutionExceptionHandler;
import org.junit.jupiter.api.extension. ExtensionContext;

import java.util.logging.Level;
import java.util.logging.Logger;

public class LoggingTestExecutionExceptionHandler implements
TestExecutionExceptionHandler {

    private Logger logger = Logger.getLogger(LoggingTestExecutionException
    Handler.class.getName());

    @Override
    public void handleTestExecutionException(ExtensionContext context,
    Throwable throwable) throws Throwable {
```

```
        logger.log(Level.INFO, "Exception thrown ", throwable);
        throw throwable;
    }
}
```

Next, you have to register your extension by annotating your test class or method with the `ExtendWith` annotation, passing it the `LoggingTestExecutionExceptionHandler` extension as shown in the following code:

```
@ExtendWith(LoggingTestExecutionExceptionHandler.class)
public class BookShelfSpecWithRules {
}
```

When you run the code, an exception will be logged as shown next.

```
bookstoread.LoggingTestExecutionExceptionHandler
handleTestExecutionException
INFO: Exception thrown
bookstoread.BookShelfCapacityReached: BookShelf capacity of 1 is reached.
You can't add more books.
        at bookstoread.BookShelf.lambda$add$0(BookShelf.java:30)
        at java.util.Spliterators$ArraySpliterator.forEachRemaining
        (Spliterators.java:948)
        at java.util.stream.ReferencePipeline$Head.forEach
        (ReferencePipeline.java:580)
        at bookstoread.BookShelf.add(BookShelf.java:28)
        at bookstoread.BookShelfSpecWithRules.throwsExceptionWhen
        BooksAreAddedAfterCapacityIsReached(BookShelfSpecWithRules.java:27)
        at sun.reflect.NativeMethodAccessorImpl.invoke0(Native Method)
        at sun.reflect.NativeMethodAccessorImpl.invoke
        (NativeMethodAccessorImpl.java:62)
        at sun.reflect.DelegatingMethodAccessorImpl.invoke
        (DelegatingMethodAccessorImpl.java:43)
        at java.lang.reflect.Method.invoke(Method.java:498)
```

Working with Test Timeout

Timeouts are useful when you don't want your test to wait indefinitely. Until the previous version of JUnit, the @Test annotation had an attribute to provide timeout value. The JUnit 5 test annotation does not support any attribute. Instead, JUnit 5 provides assertion methods that can help you deal with this situation. JUnit 5 provides extensive support for timeout.

Let's start by looking at a simple test case where we expect the test to complete in under one second.

```
@Test
void test_should_complete_in_one_second() {
    assertTimeout(Duration.of(1, ChronoUnit.SECONDS), () -> Thread.sleep(2000));
}
```

This test will fail as the code execution will sleep for two seconds. We are expecting the test case to succeed in under one second.

assertTimeout has many overload variants. The one shown previously takes two arguments–timeout duration and Executable code. When you run the test case mentioned previously, it will fail as expected. You might expect the test to fail in one second, but it will fail after two seconds.

The reason for this is that assertTimeout executes the executable code in the same thread as the calling code. This means the test will wait for the code execution to finish before raising an exception. This will lead to test failure after two seconds. On the local test machine, the test failed after 2 seconds and 40 milliseconds.

There is another set of assertTimeout overloaded methods that takes Duration and ThrowingSupplier. The difference is that ThrowingSupplier returns a value whereas Executable does not return a value. So, when you want to assert the value returned by code execution, you should use the assertTimeout ThrowingSupplier variant.

```
String message = assertTimeout(Duration.of(1, ChronoUnit.SECONDS),
() -> "Hello, World!");
assertEquals("Hello, World!", message);
```

assertTimeoutPreemptively

This method overcomes the limitation of assertTimeout. It makes sure that the test completes before the timeout. It runs the test in a different thread than the calling thread. It will abort the code when the timeout is exceeded.

```
assertTimeoutPreemptively(Duration.of(1, ChronoUnit.SECONDS),
() -> Thread.sleep(2000));
```

Now the test will finish just after the timeout duration.

Repeated Tests

JUnit 5 has added support for running a test a specified number of times. This is essential when you work with tests that are flaky in nature. Flaky tests are those that exhibit both a passing and failing behavior with the same code base. To run a test for X number of times, mark it with RepeatedTest annotation as shown in the following code:

```
@RepeatedTest(10)
void i_am_a_repeated_test() {
    assertTrue(true);
}
```

This test will run ten times and you will see the test result, as shown in the screenshot in Figure 5-1, of the integrated development environment (IDE).

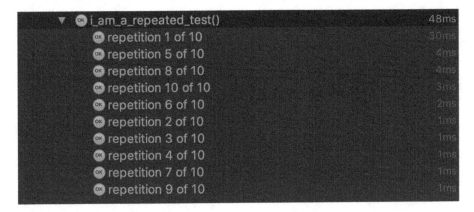

Figure 5-1. *Repeated tests execution*

You can customize the name of the test using a predefined set of placeholders.

```
@RepeatedTest(value = 10, name = "i_am_a_repeated_test__{currentRepetition}/
{totalRepetitions}")
void i_am_a_repeated_test() {
    assertTrue(true);
}
```

When you run the test, you will see following test output in your IDE as shown in the screenshot in Figure 5-2.

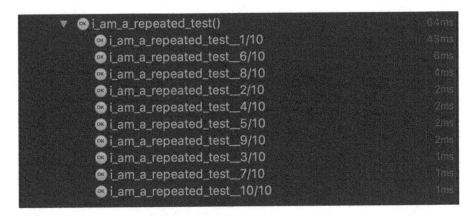

Figure 5-2. *Repeated Test with name*

Summary

In this chapter, you learned how to assert the proper behavior of tests in case of exceptions. You learned how to apply various strategies to work with the exceptions.

In Chapter 6, we will discuss how to integrate JUnit 5 with your tools. We will cover build tools, code coverage, IDE, and much more.

CHAPTER 6

■ ■ ■

Integrating Tools

Until now we have been doing development in IntelliJ Idea. We worked with various features of JUnit 5 and looked at new ways of doing things. But there are a great many tools in the Java ecosystem. There are many categories of tools—build tools, integrated develoment environment (IDE), continuous integration (CI) tools, and so on. Each of these categories offers several choices to the developer. In this chapter, we will look at ways to integrate JUnit 5 with the tool of our choice. We will first integrate JUnit 5 with the build tool of our choice. Then, we will integrate the code coverage metric. In the end, we will work with other IDE(s).

Build Tools

Build tools are responsible for automating a project build. The task of a build tool is not limited to source code compilation and binary creation. It also involves the execution of any other process like unit tests, static code analysis, binary upload, and so forth. There are many build tools in Java ecosystem, with Apache Ant, Maven, and Gradle being the ones most often adopted. For each of these tools, there is a large catalog of plug-ins that can do varied things. But in this chapter, we will focus on tasks around unit testing. The default unit testing plug-ins/extensions are based on older versions of JUnit. Thus, they are unsuitable for JUnit 5 tests. Let's look at ways we can execute JUnit 5-based tests with each of these build tools. We will start with Gradle as we have based the bookstoread application on it.

Gradle

The Gradle build tool started out by incorporating a lot of concepts from its predecessors like Ant and Maven. It takes a build.gradle file as an input to find out the steps of a project build. It is important to note that the build file is expressed in Groovy, instead of XML, which is the de facto standard for other tools. Gradle follows Maven's "*convention over configuration*" approach, where most code build practices are configured with common default values; for example, all src is kept under src/main/java and tests under src/test/java.

So far, for our project bookstoread, we added a build.gradle file (in Chapter 1). The build file describes the source code as a Java project. It also lists all the required dependencies and the repository to download dependencies from.

© Shekhar Gulati, Rahul Sharma 2017
S. Gulati, R. Sharma, *Java Unit Testing with JUnit 5*,
https://doi.org/10.1007/978-1-4842-3015-2_6

```
group 'com.junit5book'
  version '1.0-SNAPSHOT'
  apply plugin: 'java'
  sourceCompatibility = 1.8
  repositories {
      mavenCentral()
}
  dependencies {
      def junitVersion = '5.0.1'
      testCompile 'org.junit.jupiter:junit-jupiter-api:' + junitVersion
      testCompile 'org.junit.jupiter:junit-jupiter-engine:' + junitVersion
      testCompile 'org.assertj:assertj-core:3.5.2'
}
```

So, shall we try to run it on our console?

```
./gradle clean build
No command 'gradle' found
```

Ahh! we do not have gradle on our machine. But that is not an issue with Gradle. One of the most distinguishing features of Gradle is the "Gradle Wrapper." The concept is about getting a Gradle build to work without the need to install it first. It not only removes the prerequisite of Gradle installation but also forces us to have the same version of gradle on all machines it is worked upon.

The wrapper is a small script file gradlew.sh/gradlew.bat which is added to the project along with the necessary files. Let's now run the wrapper script.

```
./gradlew clean build
Downloading https://services.gradle.org/distributions/gradle-3.4.1-all.zip
..............................................................
:clean
:compileJava
:processResources UP-TO-DATE
:classes
:jar
:assemble
:compileTestJava
:processTestResources UP-TO-DATE
:testClasses
:test
:check
:build

BUILD SUCCESSFUL
```

Wow! So by using the wrapper, we were able to kick-start our build without Gradle being installed on our machine. The Gradle wrapper process downloaded the required Gradle version and project dependencies. These are then used to build the application source code. The complete build process is composed of different phases, as can be seen in the build output.

Our focus is on the test execution task. Following the concept of *sensible defaults*, Gradle adds a test plug-in to our build. The purpose of the plug-in is to execute test cases and publish a report for the same. But if we look at the build output under :test, no test cases were executed. This is because the Gradle test plug-in follows a convention that expects a test class name to end with *Test* or *Tests*. In our application, test class names ended with *Spec* so they were not executed.

Let's rerun the Gradle build by explicitly specifying that Gradle should look for classes that end with *Spec* as shown in the code that follows:

```
./gradlew clean test --tests *Spec
:test FAILED

FAILURE: Build failed with an exception.

* What went wrong:
Execution failed for task ':test'.
> No tests found for given includes: [*Spec]
```

Gradle is still unable to find our tests. This is so because JUnit 5 has changed its API (application programming interface). The JUnit 5 release is not just aimed at developers. It is also aimed at the tools/platforms based on JUnit. They have decoupled the test discovery and execution (for test filtering and configuration) required for such platforms. Since the current test plug-in is not usable, the JUnit 5 team has provided a Gradle test plug-in which could be used for executing tests.

Before we can apply the plug-in, we must tell Gradle where it can find the plug-in. This is described under the buildscript section of build.gradle.

```
buildscript {
    repositories {
        mavenCentral()
        // The following is only necessary if you want to use SNAPSHOT releases.
        // maven { url 'https://oss.sonatype.org/content/repositories/
            snapshots' }
    }
    dependencies {
        classpath 'org.junit.platform:junit-platform-gradle-plugin:1.0.1'
    }
}
apply plugin: 'org.junit.platform.gradle.plugin'
```

The `org.junit.platform.gradle.plugin`' plug-in is configured to look for tests ending in *Test(s). We must reconfigure it to discover our tests.

```
junitPlatform{
    filters{
        includeClassNamePattern '.*Spec'
    }
}
```

Now run the gradle build again, `gradle clean build`. It will run all the tests and print a test result summary on the console.

```
:junitPlatformTest
Mar 06, 2017 6:56:47 AM org.junit.platform.launcher.core.
ServiceLoaderTestEngineRegistry loadTestEngines
INFO: Discovered TestEngines with IDs: [junit-jupiter]

Test run finished after 1095 ms
[         10 containers found      ]
[          0 containers skipped    ]
[         10 containers started    ]
[          0 containers aborted    ]
[         10 containers successful ]
[          0 containers failed     ]
[         19 tests found           ]
[          0 tests skipped         ]
[         19 tests started         ]
[          0 tests aborted         ]
[         19 tests successful      ]
[          0 tests failed          ]
```

It is important to note that the plug-in will publish an XML report under 'build/test-results/junit-platform' instead of the standard Gradle test reports location (build/reports). The report is specified one per test engine.

Let's now explore the various options provided by the plug-in. By default, the plug-in discovers all the tests under the project classpath. The behavior can be changed by using the selectors block. The block enables us to limit tests to folder (s), package (s), class (es), test method (s), or any other external location.

```
junitPlatform{
    selectors{
        aClass 'bookstoread.BookShelfSpec'
    }
    filters{
        includeClassNamePattern '.*Spec'
    }
}
```

The foregoing block will only run tests of the BookShelfSpec class. It is important to note that the filters section is necessary even when we have selected only one single class. Basically, the selectors section is for the test discovery element, while the filters section is actually responsible for the test discovery.

```
Mar 06, 2017 7:53:27 AM org.junit.platform.launcher.core.
ServiceLoaderTestEngineRegistry loadTestEngines
INFO: Discovered TestEngines with IDs: [junit-jupiter]

Test run finished after 304 ms
[         6 containers found    ]
[         0 containers skipped  ]
[         6 containers started  ]
[         0 containers aborted  ]
[         6 containers successful ]
[         0 containers failed   ]
[         9 tests found         ]
[         0 tests skipped       ]
[         9 tests started       ]
[         0 tests aborted       ]
[         9 tests successful    ]
[         0 tests failed        ]
```

The filters enable us to select tests based on JUnit 5 engine, packages, tags, or class names. The following block will filter and execute tests under the Filters tag (see Chapter 4).

```
junitPlatform{
    filters{
        includeClassNamePattern '.*Spec'
        tags {
            include 'Filter'
        }
    }
}
```

The JUnit 5 Gradle platform plug-in disables the standard Gradle task. This behavior can be altered using 'enableStandardTestTask' option under the 'junitPlatform' block. Set it to "true" to enable the standard task run.

Maven

Maven was built to have a standard unified build process which can be used for any Java project. It takes an XML-based approach to configure build steps of a project (Project Object Model, or POM). As discussed earlier, it follows the convention over configuration principle, and only exceptions need to be configured explicitly. A minimalistic Maven build file 'pom.xml' contains a unique project identifier and a list of dependencies. In the following section, we will try to configure a pom.xml for our bookstoread.com.

Before we can get started we must make sure that Maven is available on our path. Unlike Gradle, it does not pack a wrapper script which could download and make it work. The latest version of Maven can be downloaded from http://maven.apache.org/. Extract the archived artifact and append it to the PATH variable. Verify if it works as expected.

```
$ mvn --version
Apache Maven 3.3.1
Maven home: /usr/share/maven
Java version: 1.8.0_101, vendor: Oracle Corporation
Java home: /usr/lib/jvm/java-8-oracle/jre
```

Now let us add the following POM file for our project:

```
<?xml version="1.0" encoding="UTF-8"?>
<project xmlns="http://maven.apache.org/POM/4.0.0">
    <modelVersion>4.0.0</modelVersion>

    <groupId>com.junit5book</groupId>
    <artifactId>bookstoread</artifactId>
    <version>1.0-SNAPSHOT</version>

    <properties>
        <project.build.sourceEncoding>UTF-8</project.build.sourceEncoding>
        <maven.compiler.source>1.8</maven.compiler.source>
        <maven.compiler.target>1.8</maven.compiler.target>
        <junit.jupiter.version>5.0.1</junit.jupiter.version>
    </properties>

    <dependencies>
        <dependency>
            <groupId>org.junit.jupiter</groupId>
            <artifactId>junit-jupiter-api</artifactId>
            <version>${junit.jupiter.version}</version>
            <scope>test</scope>
        </dependency>
        <dependency>
            <groupId>org.assertj</groupId>
            <artifactId>assertj-core</artifactId>
            <version>3.5.2</version>
            <scope>test</scope>
```

```
        </dependency>
        <dependency>
            <artifactId>mockito-core</artifactId>
            <groupId>org.mockito</groupId>
            <version>2.7.12</version>
            <scope>test</scope>
        </dependency>
    </dependencies>

</project>
```

Now we will look at the important parts.

- The project is identified by a groupId:artifactid. In addition, each released version of the project is identified by version.

- The properties section of the file lists various key values which could be referred to in the other sections of the POM.

- By default, Maven adds a Java compiler plug-in. The JDK versions for it are described by the maven.compiler.source and maven. compiler.target properties.

- The dependencies tag contains a list of dependencies required in the project, along with their respective scopes. Taking the list from the Gradle build we have added the required dependencies.

Now let us make a build:

```
$ mvn clean test
[INFO] ------------------------------------------------------------------------
----
[INFO] Building bookstoread 1.0-SNAPSHOT
[INFO] ------------------------------------------------------------------------
----
[INFO]
[INFO] --- maven-clean-plugin:2.5:clean (default-clean) @ bookstoread ---
[INFO] Deleting /home/rahul/projects/bookstoread/target
[INFO]
[INFO] --- maven-resources-plugin:2.3:resources (default-resources)
       @ bookstoread ---
[INFO] Using 'UTF-8' encoding to copy filtered resources.
[INFO] skip non existing resourceDirectory /home/rahul/projects/bookstoread/
       src/main/resources
[INFO]
[INFO] --- maven-compiler-plugin:2.0.2:compile (default-compile) @ bookstoread ---
[INFO] Compiling 4 source files to /home/rahul/projects/bookstoread/target/
       classes
[INFO]
```

```
[INFO] --- maven-resources-plugin:2.3:testResources (default-testResources)
       @ bookstoread ---
[INFO] Using 'UTF-8' encoding to copy filtered resources.
[INFO] skip non existing resourceDirectory /home/rahul/projects/bookstoread/
       src/test/resources
[INFO]
[INFO] --- maven-compiler-plugin:2.0.2:testCompile (default-testCompile)
       @ bookstoread ---
[INFO] Compiling 2 source files to /home/rahul/projects/bookstoread/target/
       test-classes
[INFO]
[INFO] --- maven-surefire-plugin:2.10:test (default-test) @ bookstoread ---
[INFO] Surefire report directory: /home/rahul/projects/bookstoread/target/
       surefire-reports


-------------------------------------------------------
 T E S T S
-------------------------------------------------------

Results :

Tests run: 0, Failures: 0, Errors: 0, Skipped: 0

[INFO] ------------------------------------------------------------------------
[INFO] BUILD SUCCESS
[INFO] ------------------------------------------------------------------------
```

But no tests ran. It is an issue similar to the one we encountered while fixing the Gradle build. Basically, the test engine is unable to find the tests, as it follows a naming convention. Thus, we need to configure the surefire plug-in to identify our tests.

```xml
<build>
    <plugins>
        <plugin>
            <artifactId>maven-surefire-plugin</artifactId>
            <version>2.19.1</version>
            <configuration>
                <includes>
                    <include>**/*Spec.java</include>
                </includes>
            </configuration>
        </plugin>
    </plugins>
</build>
```

Let us now make a build to see if it runs our tests or not.

```
[INFO] --- maven-surefire-plugin:2.19.1:test (default-test) @ bookstoread
---
-------------------------------------------------------------
 T E S T S
-------------------------------------------------------------
Running bookstoread.BookShelfSpec
Tests run: 0, Failures: 0, Errors: 0, Skipped: 0, Time elapsed: 0.004 sec -
in bookstoread.BookShelfSpec
```

As per the console output, the plug-in found the required test class but it did not find any test cases in it. Well, this is because the default plug-in is configured to work with JUnit 4. The surefire plug-in has a pluggable architecture. It can be configured by adding an additional surefireProvider to the plug-in classpath. The JUnit 5 comes with a junit-platform-surefire-provider, which can run tests based on the Jupiter engine or the Vintage engine (as per the classpath). Now let us add the provider and the Jupiter engine to the plug-in dependencies.

```
<plugin>
            <artifactId>maven-surefire-plugin</artifactId>
            <version>2.19.1</version>
            <configuration>
                <includes>
                    <include>**/*Spec.java</include>
                </includes>
            </configuration>
            <dependencies>
                <dependency>
                    <groupId>org.junit.platform</groupId>
                    <artifactId>junit-platform-surefire-provider</artifactId>
                    <version>${junit.platform.version}</version>
                </dependency>
                <dependency>
                    <groupId>org.junit.jupiter</groupId>
                    <artifactId>junit-jupiter-engine</artifactId>
                    <version>${junit.jupiter.version}</version>
                </dependency>
            </dependencies>
        </plugin>
```

Let us now make a build. All our test cases should be executed. The execution will generate output on the console as well as test files under target/surefire-reports (for later reference).

```
[INFO] --- maven-surefire-plugin:2.19.1:test (default-test) @ bookstoread ---
-------------------------------------------------------
 T E S T S
-------------------------------------------------------
Running bookstoread.BookFilterSpec
Tests run: 7, Failures: 0, Errors: 0, Skipped: 0, Time elapsed: 0.546 sec - in bookstoread.BookFilterSpec
Running bookstoread.BookShelfProgressSpec
Test info with display Name as  is 40% completed and 60% to-read when two books read and 3 books not read yet
Test info with display Name as  is 40% completed, 20% in-progress, and 40% to-read when 2 books read, 1 book in progress, and 2 books
unread
Test info with display Name as  is 0% completed and 100% to-read when no book is read yet
Tests run: 3, Failures: 0, Errors: 0, Skipped: 0, Time elapsed: 0 sec - in bookstoread.BookShelfProgressSpec
Running bookstoread.BookShelfSpec
Tests run: 9, Failures: 0, Errors: 0, Skipped: 0, Time elapsed: 0.031 sec - in bookstoread.BookShelfSpec
Running bookstoread.migration.BookShelfSpec
Tests run: 3, Failures: 0, Errors: 0, Skipped: 0, Time elapsed: 0.187 sec - in bookstoread.migration.BookShelfSpec

Results :

Tests run: 22, Failures: 0, Errors: 0, Skipped: 0
```

Figure 6-1. *Maven and JUnit 5*

The plug-in also facilitates test filtering based on tags. In order to execute/remove a set of tags specify the includeTags/excludeTags properties to the surefire plug-in configuration.

```
<configuration>
    <includes>
        <include>**/*Spec.java</include>
    </includes>
    <properties>
      <includeTags>Filter</includeTags>
    </properties>
</configuration>
```

The Maven surefire plug-in has various parameters (e.g., forkcount and parallel). These parameters are currently not supported.

Ant

Ant is one of the oldest and one of most versatile tools for project automation. It is based on a build.xml file which configures tasks that need to run on a project. Each of these tasks can be chained with other tasks to define an order of execution. Ant defines build invocation as an "arget." A project can have multiple targets which may have been chained together to define a complete build cycle. In this section, we will configure Ant to run out JUnit5-based tests as part of the project build. This section assumes knowledge of Ant.

Before we start creating a build.xml, let's make sure that we have Ant in our OS PATH. The latest version of Ant can be downloaded from http://ant.apache.org. Extract the archived artifact and append it to the PATH variable. Verify if it works as expected.

```
$ ant -version
Apache Ant(TM) version 1.9.3 compiled on April 8 2014
```

Ant has a number of extensions which can perform different tasks. Apache Ivy is one such extension which is used to perform dependency resolution. In the absence of a dependency manager, we would need to keep project dependencies as part of our source. Ivy makes it possible to express all project dependencies in an Ivy.xml. It downloads all the required dependencies when the build is executed. In order to add the ivy extension, download the latest version from http://ant.apache.org/ivy/. Extract the archive and copy the ivy.-{version}.jar to ${ ANT_HOME }/lib directory.

Now, let's add a build.xml which could do the following:

- Compile the src files.

- Compile the test files.

- Run the tests and publish a report for it.

```
<project  xmlns:ivy="antlib:org.apache.ivy.ant">

    <ivy:retrieve file="./ivy.xml" sync="true" />

    <target name="compile">
        <mkdir dir="build/classes"/>
        <javac srcdir="src/main" destdir="build/classes"/>
    </target>

    <path id="test.lib.path">
        <fileset dir="lib">
            <include name="**/*.jar" />
        </fileset>
    </path>

    <property name="test.lib" refid="test.lib.path"/>

    <target name="test-compile" depends="compile">
        <mkdir dir="build/test-classes"/>
        <javac srcdir="src/test" destdir="build/test-classes">
            <classpath>
                <path location="build/classes"/>
                <pathelement path="${test.lib}"/>
            </classpath>
        </javac>
    </target>
</project>
```

The foregoing build downloads the dependencies expressed in the ivy.xml. It then invokes the javac task to compile src. Next, it adds the downloaded libs to the classpath and invokes the javac task again to compile the test code.

```
<ivy-module version="2.0">
    <info organisation="bookstoread" module="bookstoread"/>
    <dependencies>
        <dependency org="org.junit.jupiter" name="junit-jupiter-api"
        rev="5.0.1"/>
        <dependency org="org.junit.jupiter" name="junit-jupiter-engine"
        rev="5.0.1"/>
        <dependency org="org.mockito" name="mockito-core" rev="2.7.12"/>
        <dependency org="org.assertj" name="assertj-core" rev="3.6.2"/>
    </dependencies>
</ivy-module>
```

The build only compiles code. But how do we invoke the tests? There is "junit" Ant task which can run unit tests. But the task only runs JUnit4-based test cases. Thus the task is unsuitable for our JUnit 5-based tests.

The JUnit5 team provides a console launcher which can execute tests on the console. The runner gives the process output as 1 or 0 based on a test's success or failure, respectively. The runner has a host of options to discover and execute tests. The console runner can be downloaded from maven central. Since the 1.0.1 is the currently available latest version, the same can be downloaded from http://central.maven.org/maven2/org/junit/platform/junit-platform-console-standalone/1.0.1/junit-platform-console-standalone-1.0.1.zip.

Extract the zip in our bookstoread project. Run the tests using the console launcher (see Figure 6-2) using the following command:

```
java -jar lib/junit-platform-console-standalone-1.0.1.jar --scan-classpath
-cp lib/build/classes
```

Figure 6-2. *Console launcher*

The foregoing command does the following:

- Discovers the jupiter engine which has been added to the classpath.

- '-scan-classpath' tries to find test cases which are part of the classpath.

- The command does not execute any tests as our test suffix (*spec) does not match the default convention.

110

The command provides -n option to execute classes matching the passed pattern. Thus we can add '-n "^.*Spec?$"' to discover our test cases. We would also need to add the required dependencies of assertj and mockito to the classpath.

Since the console runner can execute all our test cases, we can also add the same to our Ant build.xml. The complete approach consists of the following build steps:

1. Configure Ivy.xml to download the archive. It is important to note that we need the zip archive and not the jar (as with other dependencies).

```xml
<dependency org="org.junit.platform" name="junit-platform-
console" rev="1.0.1">
        <artifact name="junit-platform-console" type="zip"/>
    </dependency>
```

2. Extract the archive to a separate directory.

3. Execute the console runner using the exec Ant task.

4. Additionally, we can pass a -reports-dir argument to the console runner. This will create an XML-based report in the specified directory.

5. The XML-based test report can be converted to HTML by using the junitreport task.

```xml
<project default="all" xmlns:ivy="antlib:org.apache.ivy.ant">
    <property name="target.report.dir"
     value="build/test-reports"/>

    <ivy:retrieve file="./ivy.xml" sync="true" />

    <target name="clean">
        <delete dir="build"/>
    </target>

    <target name="compile">
        <mkdir dir="build/classes"/>
        <javac srcdir="src/main" destdir="build/classes"/>
    </target>

    <path id="test.lib.path">
        <fileset dir="lib">
            <include name="**/*.jar" />
        </fileset>
    </path>
```

```xml
    <property name="test.lib" refid="test.lib.path"/>

    <target name="test-compile" depends="compile">
        <mkdir dir="build/test-classes"/>
        <javac srcdir="src/test" destdir="build/test-classes">
            <classpath>
                <path location="build/classes"/>
                <pathelement path="${test.lib}"/>
            </classpath>
        </javac>
    </target>

    <target name="unit-test-runner">
        <unzip src="lib/junit-platform-console-1.0.1.zip"
        dest="lib"/>
        <chmod file="lib/junit-platform-console-1.0.1/bin/junit-
        platform-console" perm="ugo+rx"/>
    </target>

    <target name="unit-tests" depends="test-compile, unit-test-
    runner">
        <exec executable="lib/junit-platform-console-1.0.1/bin/
        junit-platform-console" >
            <arg value="-cp"/>
            <arg value="build/classes:build/test-classes:${test.
            lib}"/>
            <arg value="-scan-classpath"/>
            <arg value="-n"/>
            <arg value="^.*Spec?$"/>
            <arg value="--reports-dir"/>
            <arg value="${target.report.dir}"/>
        </exec>
    </target>

    <target name="report" depends="unit-tests">
        <mkdir dir="${target.report.dir}/html"/>
        <junitreport todir="${target.report.dir}">
            <fileset dir="${target.report.dir}">
                <include name="TEST-*.xml"/>
            </fileset>
            <report todir="${target.report.dir}/html"/>
        </junitreport>
    </target>

    <target name="all" depends="clean, unit-tests, report"></
target>

</project>
```

Code Coverage

Code coverage is an important metric captured via the execution of test cases. It is a metric expressed as a percentage of a project being tested by its test suite. There are many tools (paid and open source) which can be used to determine the coverage. Most of these tools have extensions/plug-ins which can be integrated with the project build tool. In this section, we will work with the Java Code Coverage (JaCoCo) tool. It is an open source tool, works well with all versions of Java, and integrates well with various tools like IntelliJ Idea, Gradle, Ant, Jenkins, and others. In the following section we will integrate JaCoCo with our project build.

Gradle Extension

The JaCoCo tool provides a Gradle plug-in. The plug-in is integrated with the Gradle test plug-in. But since JUnit 5 tests are not executed by the default Gradle test plug-in, so the coverage of the same cannot be determined. We need to configure jacoco with the junit-platform test plug-in provided by the JUnit 5 team. Now, let's add the plug-in to our build. gradle and try to configure it with `junitPlatformTest`.

```
apply plugin: 'jacoco'
sourceCompatibility = 1.8
repositories {
    mavenCentral()
}
// Rest removed for Brevity
jacoco {
        toolVersion = '0.7.4.201502262128'
        applyTo junitPlatformTest
    }
```

The foregoing configuration will generate a code coverage result as a binary file. We need a jacoco reporting task to convert the binary file into an xml/html report. Now, let's run the gradle build to generate coverage.

The build failed as the jacoco configuration was unable to find the required junitPlatformTest plug-in (see Figure 6-3). This is because the plug-in is not available during project initialization. It is available only after the project has been evaluated by the Gradle Runner. Now we only need to configure the jacoco plug-in in the afterEvaluted section of the project. Let's also add the jacoco reporting task; the complete configuration should look as follows:

```
afterEvaluate {
    jacoco {
        toolVersion = '0.7.4.201502262128'
        applyTo junitPlatformTest
    }
```

```
    task junit5JacocoReport(type:JacocoReport, dependsOn : junitPlatformTest){
        executionData junitPlatformTest
        sourceDirectories = files(sourceSets.main.allSource.srcDirs)
        classDirectories = files(sourceSets.main.output)
        reports {
            xml.enabled = true
            html.enabled = true
         }
    }

    build.dependsOn junit5JacocoReport

}
```

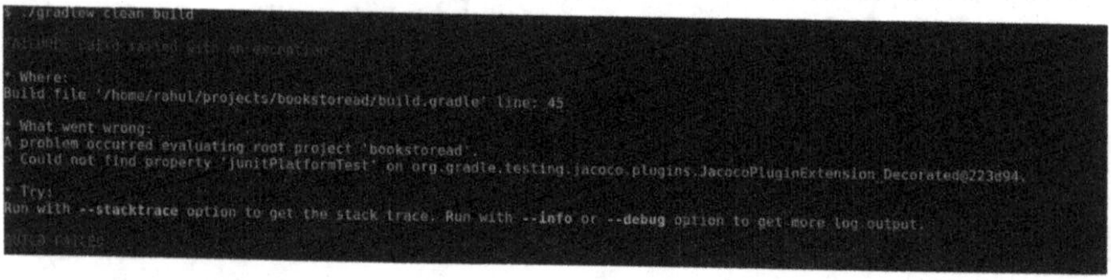

Figure 6-3. *Gradle JaCoCo failure*

Now make a build to get a `jacoco` report (see Figure 6-4).

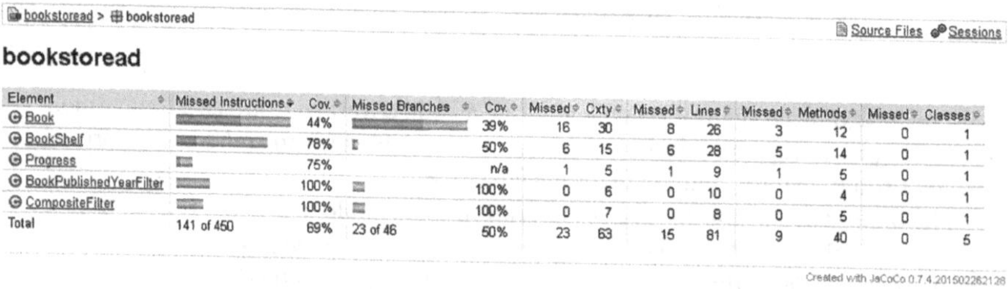
bookstoread > bookstoread

Source Files Sessions

bookstoread

Element	Missed Instructions	Cov.	Missed Branches	Cov.	Missed	Cxty	Missed	Lines	Missed	Methods	Missed	Classes
Book		44%		39%	16	30	8	26	3	12	0	1
BookShelf		78%		50%	6	15	6	28	5	14	0	1
Progress		75%		n/a	1	5	1	9	1	5	0	1
BookPublishedYearFilter		100%		100%	0	6	0	10	0	4	0	1
CompositeFilter		100%		100%	0	7	0	8	0	5	0	1
Total	141 of 450	69%	23 of 46	50%	23	63	15	81	9	40	0	5

Created with JaCoCo 0.7.4.201502262128

Figure 6-4. *Jacoco coverage report*

Maven Extension

The Maven plug-in for jacoco (jacoco-maven-plugin) works out-of-box for JUnit 5-based tests. Here also, just like Gradle, we first determine the code coverage result in a binary file and then convert it into a report. The Maven plug-in has different goals that are configured to accomplish these tasks. The following POM configuration generates a coverage report for our bookstoread.com:

```xml
<plugin>
            <groupId>org.jacoco</groupId>
            <artifactId>jacoco-maven-plugin</artifactId>
            <executions>
              <execution>
                  <id>pre-unit-test</id>
                  <goals>
                      <goal>prepare-agent</goal>
                  </goals>
                  <configuration>
                      <!-- Sets the path to the file which contains the
                      execution data. -->
                      <destFile>${project.build.directory}/coverage-
                      reports/jacoco-ut.exec</destFile>
                      <!--
                          Sets the name of the property containing the settings
                          for JaCoCo runtime agent.
                      -->
                      <propertyName>surefireArgLine</propertyName>
                  </configuration>
              </execution>
              <execution>
                  <id>post-unit-test</id>
                  <phase>test</phase>
                  <goals>
                      <goal>report</goal>
                  </goals>
                  <configuration>
                      <!-- Sets the path to the file which contains the
                      execution data. -->
                      <dataFile>${project.build.directory}/coverage-
                      reports/jacoco-ut.exec</dataFile>
                      <!-- Sets the output directory for the code coverage
                      report. -->
                      <outputDirectory>${project.reporting.
                      outputDirectory}/jacoco-ut</outputDirectory>
                  </configuration>
              </execution>
            </executions>
            </plugin>
```

Ant Extension

Now let's try to configure jacoco with Ant. As with previous configurations, here also we will determine the code coverage in two steps. The JaCoCo tool provides an Ant task which can determine code coverage by executing unit test cases or any other Java program. Since we are executing JUnit5 test cases using the console runner, we will determine the coverage by configuring a Java executable program.

Before we jump to configure jacoco, let's look into the consoleRunner script to find the complete Java command. The command executes the org.junit.platform.console. ConsoleLauncher class, with all test classes in its classpath. Now we need to configure the same command in our build script. The class is part of junit-platform-console dependency jar.

Make the following changes to the ivy.xml to make sure we download junit-platform-console jars instead of the distribution zip and the required jacoco jars:

```
<dependencies>
// Rest removed for Brevity
      <dependency org="org.junit.platform" name="junit-platform-console"
      rev="1.0.1"/>
      <dependency org="org.junit.platform" name="junit-platform-runner"
      rev="1.0.1"/>
      <dependency org="org.jacoco" name="org.jacoco.ant"
      rev="0.7.2.201409121644" />
</dependencies>
```

Now we need to configure the jacoco task with the Java main class. The following build.xml configuration makes sure that we achieve the same:

```
<project default="all" xmlns:ivy="antlib:org.apache.ivy.ant"
xmlns:jacoco="antlib:org.jacoco.ant">
    <ivy:retrieve file="./ivy.xml" sync="true" />
    // Rest removed for Brevity

    <taskdef uri="antlib:org.jacoco.ant" resource="org/jacoco/ant/antlib.xml">
        <classpath path="lib/org.jacoco.ant-0.7.2.201409121644.jar"/>
    </taskdef>

    <target name="unit-tests" depends="test-compile">
    <jacoco:coverage>
        <java classname="org.junit.platform.console.ConsoleLauncher"
        classpath="build/classes:build/test-classes:${test.lib}:${test.lib}"
        fork="true">
            <arg value="-scan-classpath"/>
            <arg value="-n"/>
            <arg value="^.*Spec?$"/>
            <arg value="--reports-dir"/>
            <arg value="${target.report.dir}"/>
        </java>
```

```
        </jacoco:coverage>
    </target>

    <target name="report" depends="unit-tests">
        <mkdir dir="${target.report.dir}/html"/>
        <junitreport todir="${target.report.dir}">
            <fileset dir="${target.report.dir}">
                <include name="TEST-*.xml"/>
            </fileset>
            <report todir="${target.report.dir}/html"/>
        </junitreport>
        <jacoco:report>
            <executiondata>
                <file file="jacoco.exec"/>
            </executiondata>
            <structure name="BooksToRead.com">
                <classfiles>
                    <fileset dir="build/classes"/>
                </classfiles>
                <sourcefiles encoding="UTF-8">
                    <fileset dir="src/main"/>
                </sourcefiles>
            </structure>
            <html destdir="${target.report.dir}/coverage"/>
        </jacoco:report>
    </target>

    <target name="all" depends="clean, unit-tests, report"></target>

</project>
```

Run the Ant build to get an html coverage report.

Other Tools

So far we have developed all our code using IntelliJ, which is constantly improving its support of JUnit 5 features. We have successfully integrated JUnit 5 with Gradle, Maven, and Ant. But the Java ecosystem contains lots of tools. There are many IDEs (Eclipse, STS, IntelliJ, NetBeans, etc.). So what do we do if the tool of our choice does not yet support JUnit5? Let's say our preferred IDE is Eclipse; so what should we do?

JUnit 5 provides a `PlatformRunner` based on JUnit 4 Runner API. The runner enables test execution on all platforms that support JUnit 4. A JUnit 5 test case must be annotated with the `@RunWith` annotation, passing the `PlatformRunner` as an argument. So now if we want to develop our code in Eclipse Neon or earlier, we do the following:

1. Add the dependency of JUnit 4 to our pom.xml or build.gradle

   ```
   testCompile 'junit:junit:4.12'
   ```

2. Add the dependency of junit-platform-runner

   ```
   testCompile 'org.junit.platform:junit-platform-runner:1.0.1'
   ```

3. Import the project into eclipse as a Gradle project (or Maven project) (see Figure 6-5)

Figure 6-5. *Eclipse import dialog*

4. Each of our test classes needs to be annotated with `@RunWith`

   ```
   @RunWith(JUnitPlatform.class)
   @DisplayName("A bookshelf")
   public class BookShelfSpec {
           private BookShelf shelf;
           // Removed  for Brevity
   }
   ```

5. Now execute our test case

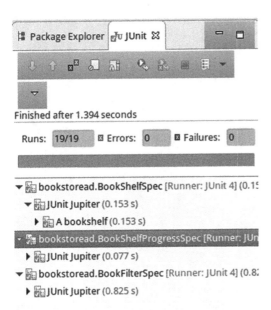

Figure 6-6. *Eclipse JUnit 5 Report*

Eclipse team is working on an Oxygen version which will contain support of JUnit 5. At the time we wrote this chapter, the Eclipse team had added JUnit 5 support [https://bugs. eclipse.org/bugs/show_bug.cgi?id=488566#c4], but it has not been released.

Summary

In this chapter, we looked at ways to configure JUnit 5 with the tools of our choice. We added Gradle-, Maven-, and Ant-based configurations to our booktoread.com. Then we generated the code coverage metric using jacoco with each of these tools. In the end, we looked at tools that do not have JUnit 5 support and configured JUnit 5 in backward-compatible mode.

In Chapter 7, we will talk about the JUnit 5 extension model and JUnit 4 migration to the newer version.

■ ■ ■

JUnit 5 Extension Model

One of the core principles of JUnit is to *prefer extension points over features*. This principle means that rather than putting all the features in the JUnit core, the JUnit team wants to offer an extensible mechanism that can be used by developers to meet their needs. This philosophy has existed in previous versions of JUnit as well. In JUnit 4, the team added support for the Rule API (application programming interface) to provide functionalities like creating temporary directories and files, exception verification, and many others. These features could have been easily added to the JUnit core without providing an extension mechanism. Instead, the JUnit team decided to build the Runner and Rule APIs, which offered a mechanism to extend JUnit. This not only enabled JUnit to build those features cleanly but also enabled third-party developers to implement their own features using the API. One such example is MockitoRule, which allows you to inject mocks into your tests.

JUnit 4 Extension Model

Before we learn about JUnit 5's new extension API let's first discuss JUnit 4's approach to extensibility. This will help us understand why the JUnit 5 team decided to design and build a new extensibility mechanism. As mentioned in the previous section, extensions are not new to JUnit. JUnit 4 offered two extension mechanisms: Runner API and Rule API.

1. **Runner API** was added to JUnit 4 to provide capability for writing custom runners. A runner manages the full life cycle of a test–instantiation of test class, calling setup and tear-down methods, executing test cases, notifying RunNotifier with progress of your tests. JUnit 4 provides an implementation, JUnit4, which is used by default. Anyone can write their own custom runner by extending the Runner class. To tell JUnit to a use custom runner, you use the @RunWith annotation and specify your custom runner as shown in the following code snippet:

   ```
   import org.junit.runner.RunWith;
   @RunWith(MyCustomRunner.class)
   public class MyTest {
   }
   ```

The two major drawbacks of the Runner API are that

    a.   Developers must implement a full life cycle even when they want to provide an extension for a specific life cycle stage. This makes it complicated and heavyweight for most use cases.

    b.   You can only use one runner class per test case. This makes them uncomposable. For example, you cannot use Parameterized and Mockito runners in the same test class.

2.   **Rule API** was introduced in JUnit 4.7 to provide a lightweight mechanism to extend JUnit. To use a rule, you create a public instance variable of the rule and annotate it with @Rule annotation. Rule API works by wrapping test methods into a statement. The statement will first run any @Before methods, then the @Test method, and finally any @After methods. The Rule API overcomes the limitations of the Runner API, but they were limited by what they could do. The main drawback of Rule APIs is that

    a.   Rule API do not control the full life cycle of the test so they can't be used for all the use cases. They only fit use cases where you need to do something before and after execution of the test case.

    b.   You have to create separate rules for method-level and class-level callbacks.

JUnit 5 Extension Model

The extension API is part of JUnit Jupiter engine. Considering the limitations of extension approaches in JUnit 4, the JUnit 5 team decided to build one unified extension API that gives the power to hook into different stages of the test life cycle. This means that when a certain life cycle phase is reached, the Jupiter engine will call all the registered extensions for that phase. There are five main extension points that you can hook into.

1.   Test life cycle callbacks

2.   Test instance post-processing

3.   Conditional test execution

4.   Parameter resolution

5.   Exception handling

Let's go through each of them in detail.

Each of the extensions covered in the subsequent sections implements interfaces corresponding to JUnit extension points. All the extension point interfaces extend a marked interface call Extension.

Another interface that you will have to interact with is ExtensionContext. It is used to encapsulate the context in which the test or test container is executed. This abstraction allows extensions to access information regarding the running test and to interact with the Jupiter engine. Let's look at the main methods of the interface to understand more about it.

```java
public interface ExtensionContext {
        Optional<ExtensionContext> getParent();
        String getUniqueId();
        String getDisplayName();
        Set<String> getTags();
        Optional<AnnotatedElement> getElement();
        Optional<Class<?>> getTestClass();
        Optional<Object> getTestInstance();
        Optional<Method> getTestMethod();
        Optional<Throwable> getExecutionException();
        void publishReportEntry(Map<String, String> map);

        default Store getStore() {
                return getStore(Namespace.DEFAULT);
        }
        Store getStore(Namespace namespace);
}
```

The getParent() method gives the ExtensionContext of the parent. To understand what "parent" means here, you have to understand that Jupiter creates a tree of test nodes and each node will have ExtensionContext. A test node will have a test class node as its parent. So, getParent will be Optional.empty when called on the test class node but it will non-empty when getParent is called on the test method.

The next set of methods gives test-unique identifiers, human-readable names, and a set of tags for a test. The next set of methods on extension makes test class, instance, and test method accessible. You can use this to reflectively access test method annotations or instance fields.

The getExecutionException() method is used to get the exception thrown during the execution of a test or container. The publishReportEntry is used to publish key/value pairs to be consumed by listeners like console or XML reports.

The last important method is getStore(). JUnit extensions make use of a Store to write and read data. Store is a namespaced, hierarchical, key/value data store. To access a store via ExtensionContext, you call the getStore method with a Namespace object. Namespace can be created using the factory method *create* like Namespace.create("com", "shekhargulati","SummaryExtension"). Each extension should use a unique namespace to avoid mixing data between different extensions.

The store itself is a glorified hash map. It offers methods that you would expect from a Map as shown in the code that follows:

```
interface Store {
  <V> V get(Object key, Class<V> requiredType);
  <K, V> Object getOrComputeIfAbsent(K key, Function<K, V> defaultCreator);
  void put(Object key, Object value);
  <V> V remove(Object key, Class<V> requiredType);
}
```

Test Life Cycle Callbacks

This set of extensions allows you to hook into specific stages of the test life cycle. As we learned in Chapter 4, the test class is composed of following life cycle methods:

1. BeforeAll: The methods marked with the @BeforeAll annotation are executed before all tests in the current test class. They are only executed once for a test class.

2. BeforeEach: The methods marked with the @BeforeEach annotation are executed before each test method in the current test class. They are called once for each test in the current test class.

3. Test: All methods marked with the @Test annotation are actual test methods.

4. AfterEach: The methods marked with @AfterEach are executed after each test method in the current test class. They are executed once for each test in the current test class.

5. AfterAll: The methods marked with @AfterAll are executed after all tests in the current test class. They are only called executed once for a test class.

For each of these test life cycle stages JUnit 5 provides an extension interface.

1. BeforeAllCallback: This extension is executed before all the test methods are executed.

2. AfterAllCallback: This extension is executed after all the test methods are executed.

3. BeforeEachCallback: This extension is executed before each test method is executed.

4. AfterEachCallback: This extension is executed after each test method is executed.

5. BeforeTestExecutionCallback: This extension is executed immediately before the test is executed.

6. AfterTestExecutionCallback: This extension is executed immediately after the test is executed.

The order of execution for a test class which has all extensions and life cycle methods is:

1. BeforeAllCallback
2. BeforeAll
3. BeforeEachCallback
4. BeforeEach
5. BeforeTestExecution
6. Test
7. AfterTestExecution
8. AfterEach
9. AfterEachCallback
10. AfterAll
11. AfterAllCallback

Let's write an extension that prints a summary of the test class execution. The summary will include the total time taken by the test class as well as the time taken by each test case. Let's start by creating our extension which implements some of the life cycle extension interfaces.

```
public class TestSummaryExtension implements
        BeforeAllCallback,
        AfterAllCallback,
        BeforeTestExecutionCallback,
        AfterTestExecutionCallback{
}
```

Each interface has a single life cycle method that we need to implement. The first method that we will implement is the beforeAll method of the BeforeAllCallback interface. We will store the start time of the test case.

```
@Override
public void beforeAll(ExtensionContext context) throws Exception {
    context.getStore().put("TEST_CLASS", System.currentTimeMillis());
}
```

Next, we will implement beforeTestExecution to store the test start time. Then, we will implement afterTestExecution to calculate the time it took to run the test case as shown in the code that follows:

```
@Override
public void beforeTestExecution(ExtensionContext context) throws Exception {
    context.getStore().put("TEST", System.currentTimeMillis());
}
```

```java
@Override
public void afterTestExecution(ExtensionContext context) throws Exception {
    long startTime = context.getStore().get("TEST", long.class);
    long timeTook = System.currentTimeMillis() - startTime;
    context.publishReportEntry(Collections.singletonMap(
            "Summary",
            String.format("%s took %d ms", context.getDisplayName(), timeTook)));
}
```

Finally, we will implement the afterAll method to calculate the time taken to run the test class and print the summary.

```java
@Override
public void afterAll(ExtensionContext context) throws Exception {
    long startTime = context.getStore().get("TEST_CLASS", long.class);
    long timeTook = System.currentTimeMillis() - startTime;
    context.publishReportEntry(Collections.singletonMap(
            "Summary",
            String.format("%s took %d ms", context.getDisplayName(), timeTook)));
}
```

To make your test use this extension, you will use the @ExtendWith annotation. We will cover it later in this chapter.

Test Instance Post-Processing

This extension allows you to hook after a test instance has been created. You implement the TestInstancePostProcessor interface. This interface has single method-postProcessTestInstance—that you should override.

As mentioned in the JavaDoc of the TestInstancePostProcessor interface, the canonical example of this extension is injecting dependencies into the test instance. For example, let's write an extension that injects SLF4j logger into an instance field.

```java
import java.lang.reflect.Field;
import org.junit.jupiter.api.extension.ExtensionContext;
import org.junit.jupiter.api.extension.TestInstancePostProcessor;
import org.slf4j.Logger;
import org.slf4j.LoggerFactory;
public class LoggingExtension implements TestInstancePostProcessor {
    @Override
    public void postProcessTestInstance(Object testInstance,
    ExtensionContext context) throws Exception {
        Logger logger = LoggerFactory.getLogger(testInstance.getClass());
        Field field = testInstance.getClass().getDeclaredField("logger");
        field.set(testInstance, logger);
    }
}
```

In the foregoing code, we have access to the testInstance. We set the logger field using reflection.

Conditional Test Execution

There are situations in which we would like to control whether we should run a test case or not. JUnit 5 provides the ExecutionCondition extension interface for implementing this use case.

Let's create an extension RunOnCIExtension class which implements the ExecutionCondition interface.

```
import org.junit.jupiter.api.extension.ConditionEvaluationResult;
import org.junit.jupiter.api.extension.ExecutionCondition;
import org.junit.jupiter.api.extension.ExtensionContext;
public class RunOnCIExtension implements ExecutionCondition {
    @Override
    public ConditionEvaluationResult evaluateExecutionCondition(ExtensionCo
ntext context) {
        String jenkinsHome = System.getenv("JENKINS_HOME");
        if (jenkinsHome != null) {
            return ConditionEvaluationResult.enabled("Test enabled on CI");
        }
        return ConditionEvaluationResult.disabled("Test disabled as the
        environment is not CI");
    }
}
```

Parameter Resolution

This extension is used to resolve a parameter received by a constructor or test method.

Let's create an extension that resolves a type Book. It is very common in the test cases that we need to work with test data. So, parameter resolution can help us there.

```
public class BookParameterResolver implements ParameterResolver {
    @Override
    public boolean supportsParameter(ParameterContext parameterContext,
      ExtensionContext extensionContext) throws ParameterResolutionException {
        return parameterContext.getParameter().getType()
          .equals(Book.class);
    }

    @Override
    public Object resolveParameter(ParameterContext parameterContext,
      ExtensionContext extensionContext) throws ParameterResolutionException {
        return new Book("Effective Java");
    }
}
```

JUnit 5 bundles the following three ParameterResolvers:

- **TestInfoParameterResolver**: The resolver provides an instance of org.junit.jupiter.api.TestInfo. The TestInfo object holds meta-information about the current test being executed. The object can provide display name, text class, test methods, and tags, if any.

- **TestReporterparameterResolver**: The resolver provides an instance of org.junit.jupiter.api.TestReporter. The TestReporter allows us to provide additional values for the current test execution. All such values are included in test report as well as shown in the IDE(s) (integrated development environment(s)).

- **RepetitionInfoParameterResolver**: The resolver provides an instance of org.junit.jupiter.api.RepetitionInfo. The RepetitionInfo object holds information about the test repetition (i.e., current repetition index and total repetitions). The object is only available for tests annotated with org.junit.Jupiter.api.RepeatedTest. If the test case is not marked with @RepeatedTest, an org.junit.jupiter.api.extension.ParameterResolutionException is thrown.

```
class ParameterResolverSpec {

    @BeforeEach
    void initialize(TestInfo info,TestReporter reporter) {
        reporter.publishEntry("Associated tags :", info.getTags().
toString());
    }

    @RepeatedTest(value = 10)
    @Tag("Numbers")
    void numberTest(RepetitionInfo info) {
        assertTrue(true);
    }

    @Test
    void nonRepeated(RepetitionInfo info) {
        assertTrue(true);
    }
}
```

TestReporter is Junit 5's preferred way to print any information to sysout/syserror. Also note that each of the aforementioned ParameterResolver(s) is activated automatically by the JUnit execution engine. They do not require any explicit activation using @ExtendsWith.

Exception Handling

The last extension point that we will discuss is TestExecutionExceptionHandler. This extension can be used to alter the behavior of a test when it encounters an exception.

Let's suppose, we want to create an extension that will log and ignore all exceptions of type IOException and rethrow all the other exceptions.

```
public class IgnoreIOExceptionExtension
  implements TestExecutionExceptionHandler {
    Logger logger = LoggerFactory
      .getLogger(IgnoreIOExceptionExtension.class);
    @Override
    public void handleTestExecutionException(ExtensionContext context,
      Throwable throwable) throws Throwable {

        if (throwable instanceof IOException) {
            logger.error("IO Exception {}", throwable);
            return;
        }
        throw throwable;
    }
}
```

Registering Extensions

In the previous few sections, we created our test extensions. Now, we need to register them with a JUnit 5 test. To do that, we make use of the @ExtendWith annotation. You can use this annotation multiple times to register multiple extensions or you can pass multiple extensions as an array to the @ExtendWith annotation.

```
@ExtendWith({
    IgnoreIOExceptionExtension.class,
    BookParameterResolver.class,
    RunOnCIExtension.class,
    TestSummaryExtension.classs
})
@ExtendWith(LoggingExtension.class)
public class UserServiceTests{

}
```

You can also automatically register extensions by using the ServiceLoader mechanism. Your extension needs to have a file META-INF/services/org.junit.jupiter.api. extension.Extension with the fully qualified name of your extension.

```
com.shekhargulati.extensions.TestSummaryExtension.
```

To enable this extension registry mechanism, you will need to set the junit. extensions.autodetection.enabled configuration property to true. One way to do this is by using a system property to the JVM (Java Virtual Machine). The other way is by adding a configuration parameter to LauncherDiscoveryRequest as shown in the code that follows:

```
LauncherDiscoveryRequest request
  = LauncherDiscoveryRequestBuilder.request()
  .selectors(selectClass("com.junit5book.UserServiceTests"))
  .configurationParameter("junit.extensions.autodetection.enabled", "true")
.build();
```

JUnit 5 Extensions

The JUnit team used the extension model to develop the following new test types:

- @TestTemplate: Define a template which generates tests at runtime.

- @ParametrerizedTest: Defines a test method with parameters.

In the following sections we will cover how to use each of the aforementioned extensions. The sections will not cover implementation details for each of the extensions. Please refer to JUnit 5 documentation for such details.

Test Template

JUnit 5 enables us to create test skeletons which are instantiated with TestTemplateInvocationContext to generate tests at runtime. The generated tests are like @Test method. The templates support the complete test life cycle. Any methods annotated with @BeforeAll/@BeforeEach/@AfterEach/@AfterAll are executed as per life cycle for the generated test.

A test template is created by marking a non-static method test class with org. junit.jupiter.api.TestTemplate annotation. Additionally, we must register an implementation of TestTemplateInvocationContextProvider Extension, which is used to generate an actual test from the template.

Let's try to add a test template for our bookstoread application. In Chapter 4, we added BookFilter which could be applied to a Book. The filter validates if the book meets a criterion. We also created BookPublishedYearFilter, which can be used to filter a book based on the year of publishing.

In the current context let's add a test template which could take BookFilter and an array of books and then assert the filter validation.

```
class BookFilterTemplateSpec {

    @TestTemplate
    @ExtendWith(BookFilterTestInvocationContextProvider.class)
    void validateFilters(BookFilter filter, Book[] books) {
        assertNotNull(filter);
```

```
        assertFalse(filter.apply(books[0]));
        assertTrue(filter.apply(books[1]));
    }
}
```

As shown in the foregoing test case we also need to create a
BookFilterTestInvocationContextProvider, an implementation of org.junit.jupiter.api.
extension.TestTemplateInvocationContextProvider. The provider needs to implement the
following methods:

supportsTestTemplate: The method validates if the provider is applicable for the
passed ExecutionContext. The JUnit execution engine first calls this method to validate if
the provider is applicable or not.

provideTestTemplateInvocationContexts: The method provides a Stream of
org.junit.jupiter.api.extension.TestTemplateInvocationContext. Each instance of
TestTemplateInvocationContext is responsible for providing a corresponding test name
and additional extensions, if any.

```
class BookFilterTestInvocationContextProvider implements
TestTemplateInvocationContextProvider {
    @Override
    public boolean supportsTestTemplate(ExtensionContext context) {
        return true;
    }

    @Override
    public Stream<TestTemplateInvocationContext> provideTestTemplateInvocati
onContexts(ExtensionContext context) {
        Book cleanCode = new Book("Clean Code", "Robert C. Martin",
        LocalDate.of(2008, Month.AUGUST, 1));
        Book codeComplete = new Book("Code Complete", "Steve McConnel",
        LocalDate.of(2004, Month.JUNE, 9));
        return Stream.of(bookFilterTestContext("Before Filter",
        BookPublishedYearFilter.Before(2007), cleanCode, codeComplete),
                bookFilterTestContext("After Filter",
                BookPublishedYearFilter.After(2007), codeComplete,
                cleanCode));
    }

    private TestTemplateInvocationContext bookFilterTestContext(String
testName, BookFilter bookFilter, Book... array) {
        return new TestTemplateInvocationContext() {
            @Override
            public String getDisplayName(int invocationIndex) {
                return testName;
            }
```

131

```
            @Override
            public List<Extension> getAdditionalExtensions() {
                return Lists.newArrayList(new TypedParameterResolver
                (bookFilter), new TypedParameterResolver(array));
            }
        };
    }
}
```

Let's look at the provideTestTemplateInvocationContexts method in detail. The method returns a Stream<TestTemplateInvocationContext>. Each instance of TestTemplateInvocationContext provides a test display name and two additional extensions. These extensions are responsible for resolving method parameters for our validateFilters test.

Our BookFiltertestInvocationContextProvider generates the following two test cases:

- **Before Year Test**: The test contains the BookPublishedYearFilter. Before(2007) filter and an array of two books.

- **After Year Test**: The test contains the BookPublishedYearFilter. After(2007) filter and an array of two books.

We have added a TypedParameterResolver extension. The extension takes a value and validates if it is an instance of one of the passed method arguments. If so, it provides back the value.

```
class TypedParameterResolver<T> implements ParameterResolver {
    T data;

    TypedParameterResolver(T data) {
        this.data = data;
    }

    @Override
    public boolean supportsParameter(ParameterContext parameterContext,
    ExtensionContext extensionContext) throws ParameterResolutionException {
        Class parameterClass = parameterContext.getParameter().getType();
        return parameterClass.isInstance(data);
    }

    @Override
    public Object resolveParameter(ParameterContext parameterContext,
    ExtensionContext extensionContext) throws ParameterResolutionException {
        return data;
    }
}
```

Now that we have added all the required components for our test template, let's execute it. There will be two tests, one doing the "before year" check and the other doing the "after year" check (see Figure 7-1).

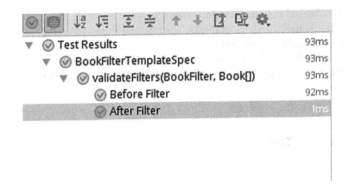

Figure 7-1. *Test template result*

Parameterized Test

In Chapter 4, we found out that JUnit 5 allows us to inject parameters into a test. The parameter can be injected into the test method or the BeforeEach/AfterEach methods. This is accomplished by implementing the org.juint.jupiter.extension.Extension interface, which could provide the value, and then registering it for the test by using @ExtendWith.

But in case we need to inject values into the test method ONLY, we can do away with the custom implementation of org.juint.jupiter.extension.Extension. Instead we can annotate the test method with org.junit.jupiter.params.ParameterizedTest. We would also need to register a ValueSource, which is used to provide values.

In our bookstoread application, we added a findBookByTitle method to our Bookshelf. Let's add a test case where we would search our bookshelf for an existing title.

```
@ParameterizedTest
@ValueSource(strings = {"Effective Java", "Code Complete", "Clean Code"})
void shouldGiveBackBooksForTitle(String title) {
    BookShelf shelf = new BookShelf();
    Book effectiveJava = new Book("Effective Java", "Joshua Bloch",
    LocalDate.of(2008, Month.MAY, 8));
    Book codeComplete = new Book("Code Complete", "Steve McConnel",
    LocalDate.of(2004, Month.JUNE, 9));
    Book mythicalManMonth = new Book("The Mythical Man-Month", "Frederick
    Phillips Brooks", LocalDate.of(1975, Month.JANUARY, 1));
    Book cleanCode = new Book("Clean Code", "Robert C. Martin", LocalDate.
    of(2008, Month.AUGUST, 1));
    shelf.add(effectiveJava, codeComplete, mythicalManMonth, cleanCode);
    List<Book> foundBooks = shelf.findBooksByTitle(title.toLowerCase());
    assertNotNull(foundBooks);
    assertEquals(1,foundBooks.size());
    foundBooks = shelf.findBooksByTitle(title.toUpperCase());
    assertNotNull(foundBooks);
    assertEquals(0,foundBooks.size());
}
```

The shouldGiveBackBooksForTitle test method takes a String as an input. The method then constructs a BookShelf with a list of Books. The test case then asserts the specified title using the findBooksByTitle method.

The String parameter value is specified by @ValueSource, used on the test method. The annotation takes a string array as an input and thus repeats the test for each value (see Figure 7-2).

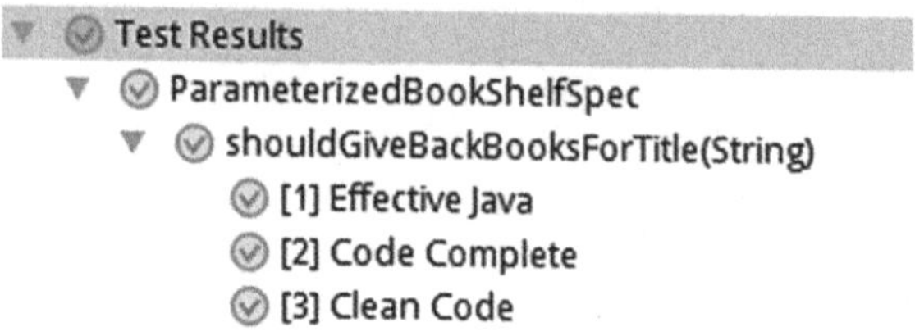

Figure 7-2. *String parameters*

@ValueSource can be used to specify an array of primitive (integer/double/long) and String. The package also provides the following sources:

- **EnumSource**: The source can be used to inject values from an Enum. The source allows to select/deselect a subset of specified Enum values.

- **MethodSource**: The source can be used provide a Stream/Array/ Iterable of values. The method must be static and must not take any arguments.

- **CSVSource**: The source can be used to inject a list of comma separated values. Each of the comma separated values can be used to match a test method argument.

- **CSVFileSource**: The source can be used to inject a list of comma separated values from a specified file. Each of the comma separated values can be used to match a test method argument.

- ArgumentSource: The source can be used to register a custom provider of Stream<Arguments>. The registered provider can be used to inject custom types, or multiple arguments (in pairs).

Now, let's use some of these sources for our bookstoread application. We can use a MethodSource to provide us an array of BookFilters, which can be validated in isolation.

```
@ParameterizedTest
@MethodSource("bookFilterProvider")
void validateFilterWithNullData(BookFilter filter) {
    assertThat(filter.apply(null)).isFalse();
}

static Stream<BookFilter> bookFilterProvider() {
    return Stream.of(BookPublishedYearFilter.Before(2007),
    BookPublishedYearFilter.After(2007));
}
```

We could also register a Custom provider which can inject values in pairs. This can be used to simplify our BookFilter template test created in the previous section. Here as well, the test method will take a BookFilter and Book[] as an argument. It then validates the values of Book[] using the provided filter.

```
@ParameterizedTest
@ArgumentsSource(BookFilterCompositeArgsProvider.class)
void validateBookFiltersWithBooks(BookFilter filter, Book[] books) {
    assertNotNull(filter);
    assertFalse(filter.apply(books[0]));
    assertTrue(filter.apply(books[1]));
}
class BookFilterCompositeArgsProvider implements ArgumentsProvider {
    @Override
    public Stream<? extends Arguments> provideArguments(ExtensionContext
    context) {
        Book cleanCode = new Book("Clean Code", "Robert C. Martin",
        LocalDate.of(2008, Month.AUGUST, 1));
        Book codeComplete = new Book("Code Complete", "Steve McConnel",
        LocalDate.of(2004, Month.JUNE, 9));
        return Stream.of(Arguments.of(BookPublishedYearFilter.Before(2007),
        Arrays.array(cleanCode, codeComplete)),
                Arguments.of(BookPublishedYearFilter.After(2007), Arrays.
                array(codeComplete, cleanCode)));
    }
}
```

The BookFilterCompositeArgsProvider provides a stream of arguments, where each instance of argments consists of two values (i.e., a BookFilter and a Book[]).

All of the previously discussed sources are repeatable. A test can have multiple annotations, which could provide different sets of values. In the following test case we have replaced Book[] with an instance of a Book. Thus the test method takes a BookFilter and a Book as an argument. The test is annotated with BeforeYearArgsProvider, for values satisfying criteria for a BeforePublishedYear filter, and AfterYearArgsProvider, for values satisfying the AfterPublishYear filter.

```
@ParameterizedTest(name = "{index} : Validating {1}")
@DisplayName("Filter validates a passing book")
@ArgumentsSource(BeforeYearArgsProvider.class)
@ArgumentsSource(AfterYearArgsProvider.class)
void validateBookFiltersWithBooks1(BookFilter filter, Book book) {
    assertNotNull(filter);
    assertTrue(filter.apply(book));
}
}
class BeforeYearArgsProvider implements ArgumentsProvider {
    @Override
    public Stream<? extends Arguments> provideArguments(ExtensionContext
    context) {
        Book cleanCode = new Book("Clean Code", "Robert C. Martin",
        LocalDate.of(2006, Month.AUGUST, 1));
        Book codeComplete = new Book("Code Complete", "Steve McConnel",
        LocalDate.of(2004, Month.JUNE, 9));
        return Stream.of(Arguments.of(BookPublishedYearFilter.Before(2007),
        cleanCode),
                Arguments.of(BookPublishedYearFilter.Before(2007),
                codeComplete));
    }
}
class AfterYearArgsProvider implements ArgumentsProvider {

    @Override
    public Stream<? extends Arguments> provideArguments(ExtensionContext
    context) {
        Book cleanCode = new Book("Clean Code", "Robert C. Martin",
        LocalDate.of(2009, Month.AUGUST, 1));
        Book codeComplete = new Book("Code Complete", "Steve McConnel",
        LocalDate.of(2008, Month.JUNE, 9));
        return Stream.of(Arguments.of(BookPublishedYearFilter.After(2007),
        cleanCode),
                Arguments.of(BookPublishedYearFilter.After(2007),
                codeComplete));
    }
}
```

Now, in the foregoing code we have used @DisplayName. The annotation gives a meaning name to the complete test execution (consisting of all passed values). Additionally, each test execution can be provided a meaningful name by specifying the name attribute of @ParametrizedTest. In case we do not provide any name, the test execution generates a default name by using the injected values. Let's now run our complete test (see Figure 7-3).

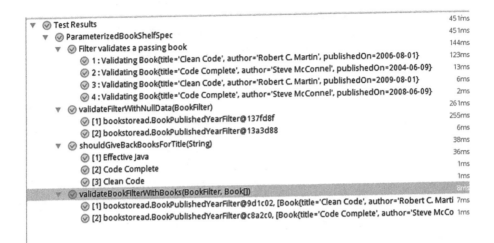

Figure 7-3. *Parameterized test result*

Summary

In this chapter, we started our discussion by learning about JUnit 5's new extension API. We discovered that the extension API supports all life cycle phases of test execution. The API also supports conditional test execution as well as exceptions generated during test execution. The JUnit 5 package uses the extension API to provide a host of features like default providers, test templates, and parameterized tests.

■ ■ ■

CHAPTER 8

Dynamic Tests and Migration from JUnit 4

In the book, so far, we have learned about different features of JUnit 5 by building tests for our bookstoread application. All tests that we have added thus far have been static in nature. JUnit 5 offers us a new paradigm of runtime test creation. In this chapter, we will look at dynamic test generation.

We have addressed all the features of JUnit 5. We can now say that JUnit 5 is going to be the de facto standard for unit testing in the future. Various tools and platform are in the process of building support for JUnit 5. We can jump on the JUnit 5 bandwagon and start adopting it. But in the past, we developed lots of tests and utilities on JUnit 4, which are still delivering value to us. We could keep all that code from the older tooling/ infrastructure. But that would make things difficult as we proceed further. In this chapter, we will also look at ways to migrate all our existing JUnit 4-based code to the new version.

Dynamic Tests

Until now we have experienced a couple of ways (@Test, @TestTemplate, @ParameterizedTest) to create a test case. All of these methods define tests which are static in nature. The behavior defined in such tests is compile time defined and cannot be altered at runtime. Assumptions allow us to add some runtime behavior. But they are also limited in the capability they offer. JUnit 5 introduces @TestFactory, a dynamic model of test execution. The model enables us to generate test cases at runtime. The model is quite useful in scenarios where we expect different behaviors based on environment, operating system, parameters, application configuration, and so on. A method annotated with @TestFactory must return a Stream/Collection/Iterable/Iterator of DynamicTest. An attempt to return anything else will result in org.junit.platform.commons.JUnitException. The org.junit. jupiter.api.DynamicTest class consists of a test name and an executable which must be executed as part of the test execution.

```
public class DynamicSpec {

    @TestFactory
    Collection<DynamicTest> generateFirstTest() {
```

© Shekhar Gulati, Rahul Sharma 2017
S. Gulati, R. Sharma, *Java Unit Testing with JUnit 5*,
https://doi.org/10.1007/978-1-4842-3015-2_8

```
  return Arrays.asList(
    dynamicTest("Week Test", () -> assertEquals(DayOfWeek.
    MONDAY,DayOfWeek.of(1))),
    dynamicTest("Month Test", () -> assertEquals(Month.JANUARY, Month.
    of(1)))
  );
}

}
```

A dynamic test has a completely different life cycle when compared to a static test. There are no callback/life cycle methods. Also, these tests do not support the JUnit 5 extension model. As a result, we cannot inject any parameters using the extension model. But Java 8 lambda expressions allow us to pass a single method argument to the respective dynamically generated tests. There is a DynamicTest.stream API (application programming interface) which enables us to pass an iterator of input parameters. Each value retrieved from the iterator is passed to a new test execution.

```
@TestFactory
Stream<DynamicTest> generateParameterizedTest() {
  LocalDate startDate = LocalDate.now();
  Iterator<LocalDate> daysIter = Stream.iterate(startDate, date -> date.
  plusDays(1)).limit(10).iterator();
  return  stream(daysIter, d -> DateTimeFormatter.ISO_LOCAL_DATE.format(d),
  d -> assertNotNull(d));
}
```

Let's run DynamicSpec. We should see a green bar with 12 test cases being executed. We have discussed the fact that dynamic tests do not have test life cycle and extension support. But this does not mean that we cannot use these features with a dynamic test. The @TestFactory method, responsible for generating tests, supports all these features. We can register an extension to inject values into the @TestFactory method.

```
@TestFactory
@ExtendWith(BooksProvider.class)
Stream<DynamicTest> generateBooksTest(Book[] books) {
  return  stream(Arrays.<Book>asList(books).iterator(), b  -> String.format
  ("Validating : %s",b.getTitle()), b -> assertFalse(b.isProgress()));
}
```

The foregoing test method injects a Book[] using BooksProvider, added in Chapter 4. The generated tests will contain a book name as part of the test name.

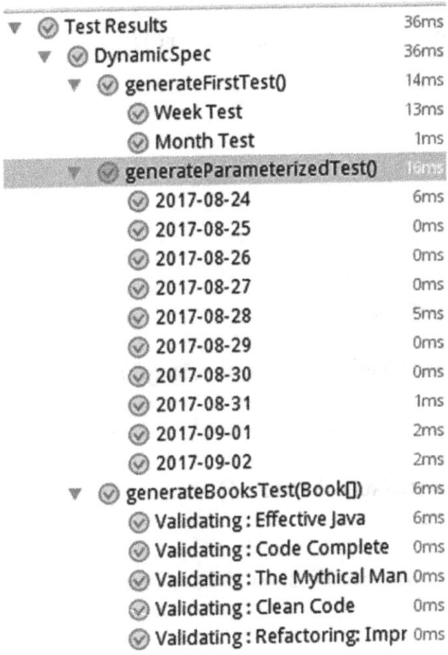

▼ ⊘ Test Results		36ms
▼ ⊘ DynamicSpec		36ms
▼ ⊘ generateFirstTest()		14ms
⊘ Week Test		13ms
⊘ Month Test		1ms
▼ ⊘ generateParameterizedTest()		16ms
⊘ 2017-08-24		6ms
⊘ 2017-08-25		0ms
⊘ 2017-08-26		0ms
⊘ 2017-08-27		0ms
⊘ 2017-08-28		5ms
⊘ 2017-08-29		0ms
⊘ 2017-08-30		0ms
⊘ 2017-08-31		1ms
⊘ 2017-09-01		2ms
⊘ 2017-09-02		2ms
▼ ⊘ generateBooksTest(Book[])		6ms
⊘ Validating : Effective Java		6ms
⊘ Validating : Code Complete		0ms
⊘ Validating : The Mythical Man		0ms
⊘ Validating : Clean Code		0ms
⊘ Validating : Refactoring: Impr		0ms

Figure 8-1. *Dynamic tests*

JUnit 4 Support

JUnit 5 is a rewrite of the framework based on lessons learned in the past. It offers us new and simple ways to accomplish things. It has built a new programming model and an extensions framework that is not compatible with older versions of the framework. Even though the new version is not compatible with the older version, the framework writers have made sure that the new and the old versions can coexist within the same infrastructure. They have built enough support so that developers can have an easy migration path.

Let's start by adding a sample JUnit 4-based test to our bookstoread project. In Chapter 1 we added BookShelfSpec. The test cases define the behavior for the BookShelf class under various scenarios. Now, add a new test case bookstoread.junit4. BookShelfSpec.

```
@RunWith(MockitoJUnitRunner.class)
public class BookShelfSpec {
  private BookShelf shelf;
  @Mock
  private Book effectiveJava;
  @Mock
  private Book codeComplete;
```

```java
@Rule
public TemporaryFolder temporaryFolder = new TemporaryFolder();

@Before
public void init() throws Exception{
  shelf = new BookShelf();
  temporaryFolder.newFile();
}

@Test
public void emptyBookShelfWhenNoBookAdded() {
  List<Book> books = shelf.books();
  assertTrue(books.isEmpty(), () -> "BookShelf should be empty");
}

@Test
public void bookshelfContainsTwoBooksWhenTwoBooksAdded() {
  shelf.add(effectiveJava, codeComplete);
  List<Book> books = shelf.books();
  assertEquals(2, books.size(), () -> "BookShelf should have two books");
}
}
```

In the foregoing test case, our test annotations are from the org.juint package. To use this package we must add testCompile junit:junit:4.12 dependency in our build.gradle

In the foregoing test case, we have added features of JUnit 4 like Runners and Rules, even though a few of them are not required. The aim here is to determine how we can work with all these features.

Let's try a ./gradlew clean build to have a successful build. Our bookstoread application source code has a junitPlatformTest plug-in. The plug-in by default disables the standard Gradle test task. Enable it by adding the following configuration:

```
junitPlatform{
      enableStandardTestTask true
}
```

We would also configure the test plug-in for the bookstoread.junit4 package.

```
test {
    include '**/junit4/**'
}
```

A build should give us the test execution report in the build/reports folder (see Figure 8-2):

Test Summary

Package	Tests	Failures	Ignored	Duration	Success rate
bookstoread.junit4	3	0	0	0.031s	100%

Figure 8-2. JUnit 4 tests

Using Vintage Engine

The next version of JUnit not only refines the testing APIs but also defines a platform framework which could be used by the various tools/plug-ins built on top of JUnit. The platform framework bundles tooling APIs, which are aimed at test discovery, filtration, reporting, and so on. It also defines a pluggable engine which is responsible for executing tests. This allows us to have separate engines which would execute different kinds of tests. The JUnit 5 version defines the Jupiter engine to execute tests based on the JUnit 5 API. It also defines a Vintage engine to execute tests based on older versions of JUnit.

The JunitPlatformTest plug-in is based on the previously described framework. The plug-in discovers the engines available in the project classpath and executes them. Until now we have been using Jupiter engine only. The Vintage engine can be enabled by adding it to our build.gradle.

```
testCompile 'org.junit.vintage:junit-vintage-engine:4.12.1'
```

Now a ./gradlw clean build should provide a test execution report in the build/test-results/junit-platform folder. The folder will have an XML report for each of the engines executed.

```
<testcase time="0.109" name="bookshelfContainsTwoBooksWhenTwoBooksAdded"
classname="bookstoread.junit4.BookShelfSpec">
<system-out>
<![CDATA[ unique-id: [engine:junit-vintage]/[runner:bookstoread.
junit4.BookShelfSpec]/[test:bookshelfContainsTwoBooksWhenTwo
BooksAdded(bookstoread.junit4.BookShelfSpec)] display-name:
bookshelfContainsTwoBooksWhenTwoBooksAdded ]]>
</system-out>
</testcase>
```

The Vintage engine is a seamless way to integrate all the existing JUnit 4-based code. It is important to note that using Vintage engine will help test cases based on different versions of JUnit to coexist in the same project. But this does not make older versions of the tests use the new features/aspects of JUnit 5. As shown in the JUnit execution report in Figure 8-3, the two engines are executed independently of each other.

bookstoread in bookstoread_test: 22 total, 22 passed			204 ms

Collapse | Expand

JUnit Vintage			109 ms
bookstoread.junit4.BookShelfSpec			109 ms
bookshelfContainsTwoBooksWhenTwoBooksAdded		passed	94 ms
emptyBookShelfWhenNoBookAdded		passed	15 ms
emptyBookShelfWhenAddIsCalledWithoutBooks		passed	0 ms
JUnit Jupiter			95 ms
Filter based on			63 ms
progress			0 ms
A bookshelf			32 ms
books are grouped by			32 ms
is arranged			0 ms
after adding books			0 ms
is empty			0 ms

Figure 8-3. *Combined engine report*

Moving to JUnit 5

The Vintage engine offers migration flexibility to developers. We can start with it, thus building all our test cases with the new ecosystem and then slowly moving our tests to the new JUnit 5 API. The new API exists under the org.junit.jupiter.api package. Most of the test life cycle annotations have a one-to-one mapping between the older version and the new version.

Junit 4 (org.juint)	Junit 5 (org.junit.jupiter.api)
Test	Test
Before	BeforeEach
BeforeClass	BeforeAll
After	AfterEach
AfterClass	AfterAll
Ignore	Disabled
Category	Tag
RunWith	ExtendWith

In order to migrate our existing JUnit 4-based bookstoread.junit4.BookShelfSpec test we must do the following:

- Replace all the old test annotations with their corresponding new value.

- Refactor the test cases for the JUnit 4 assertions. Some of the JUnit 4 assertions are no longer supported. In the new version all assertions are part of org.junit.jupiter.api.Assertions class.

- Refactor the test cases for the JUnit 4 assumptions. Some of the JUnit 4 assumptions are no longer supported. In the new version all assumptions are part of org.junit.jupiter.api.Assumptions class.

- The RunWith annotation takes a MockitoJunit4Runner class.
  But the same cannot be used with ExtendWith. The Runner
  model of JUnit 4 is no longer supported in the new version.
  Instead of the Runners, the new version asks for extensions.
  These extensions need to be added to the new versions of each
  framework (e.g., Mockito needs to have a MockitoExtension). In
  a similar manner, when we work with Spring-based applications
  we have a SpringJUnit4ClassRunner, to inject dependencies via
  spring context. The same runner cannot be used with JUnit 5;
  thus Spring developers have added a SpringExtension, currently
  developed under Spring 5.0-SNAPSHOT.

- The RunWith annotation can be applied only once to a test class.
  Thus, only a single Runner can be applied to a test class. But
  the ExtendWith annotation does not have this limitation. It is a
  repeatable annotation, which allows a test class to have multiple
  extensions.

- In case the extension is not available, as in our case, we need to
  perform the same task, (i.e., creating mocks) in our test case.

- JUnit 4 introduced Rules, which can be used to add behaviors to
  each test case. There are two kinds of annotations for Rules.

  - @Rule, executed for each test.

  - @ClassRule, executed once for all tests in a test class.

  In the new version, both of these are not supported anymore.
  Instead of Rules, developers should extend behaviors by using
  extensions. But there are many kinds of Rules, for all kind of
  things, like adding temporary files, timeouts, StopWatch, and
  so on. Thus, all of them need to be refactored to the new
  model, but does that mean we have lost the functionality? The
  JUnit 5 team has provided specific extensions to make sure all
  the existing Rules work without any changes. The following
  extensions have been added to JUnit 5:

  - ExternalResourceSupport

  - VerifierSupport

  - ExpectedExceptionSupport

We can add each of them to our test cases, or alternatively we have the
EnableRuleMigrationSupport annotation, which can enable all of them. These
extensions are part of the junit-jupiter-migration support component. Thus we need to
add the same to our build.gradle:

```
testCompile 'org.junit.jupiter:junit-jupiter-migrationsupport:5.0.1'
```

In the end, our migrated test case looks as follows:

```
@EnableRuleMigrationSupport
class BookShelfSpec {
  private BookShelf shelf;
@Mock
  private Book effectiveJava;
@Mock
 private Book codeComplete;

  @Rule
  public TemporaryFolder temporaryFolder = new TemporaryFolder();

  @BeforeEach
  void init() throws Exception {
    shelf = new BookShelf();
    MockitoAnnotations.initMocks(this);
    temporaryFolder.newFile();
  }

  @Test
  void emptyBookShelfWhenNoBookAdded() {
    List<Book> books = shelf.books();
    assertTrue(books.isEmpty(), () -> "BookShelf should be empty");
  }
}
```

In JUnit 5, if we run rules without the corresponding extension, the execution engine gives all kinds of exceptions while executing the rule methods. The exceptions are mostly around logic written in rules rather generic JUnit 5 errors.

The foregoing test case no longer requires the Vintage engine for test execution. But we still cannot remove its dependency. The test case is using the Temporary folder rule, which is part of JUnit 4.

Run a ./gradlew clean build to make sure all tests are green, as in the report in Figure 8-4.

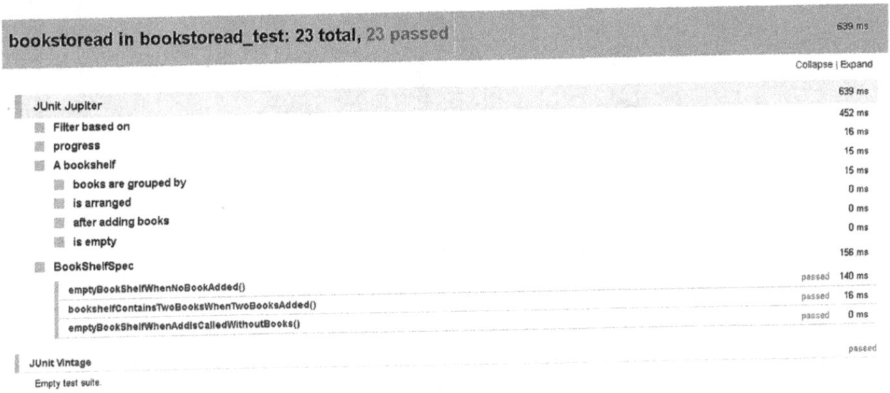

bookstoread in bookstoread_test: 23 total, 23 passed	639 ms
	Collapse | Expand
	639 ms
JUnit Jupiter	452 ms
Filter based on	16 ms
progress	15 ms
A bookshelf	15 ms
books are grouped by	0 ms
is arranged	0 ms
after adding books	0 ms
is empty	156 ms
BookShelfSpec	
emptyBookShelfWhenNoBookAdded()	passed 140 ms
bookshelfContainsTwoBooksWhenTwoBooksAdded()	passed 16 ms
emptyBookShelfWhenAddIsCalledWithoutBooks()	passed 0 ms
	passed
JUnit Vintage	
Empty test suite.	

Figure 8-4. Vintage to Jupiter

Summary

In this chapter, we learned how we can migrate all our existing tests to the new version. JUnit 5 defines a platform framework, which allows us to have pluggable engines for test execution. Tests based on the JUnit 5 API are executed by the Jupiter engine and tests based on older version of JUnit are executed by the Vintage engine. These two engines allow us to have tests based on the new and the old JUnit APIs in the same project. But this does not enable the old version of the tests to use the new features offered in JUnit 5. If we want to use them the tests need to be migrated to the new version. Finally, we listed the important things we need to consider while doing a migration to JUnit 5.

Index

© Shekhar Gulati, Rahul Sharma 2017
S. Gulati, R. Sharma, *Java Unit Testing with JUnit 5*,
https://doi.org/10.1007/978-1-4842-3015-2

Get the eBook for only $5!

Why limit yourself?

With most of our titles available in both PDF and ePUB format, you can access your content wherever and however you wish—on your PC, phone, tablet, or reader.

Since you've purchased this print book, we are happy to offer you the eBook for just $5.

To learn more, go to http://www.apress.com/companion or contact support@apress.com.

Apress®

Printed in the United States
By Bookmasters